PRAISE FOR THE UNEMPLOYED COLLEGE GRADUATE'S SURVIVAL GUIDE

"*The Unemployed College Graduate's Survival Guide* manages to be both optimistic and realistic. Dr. Snyder doesn't sugarcoat the predicament faced by today's young graduates, but she also doesn't let them sulk. The result is a sympathetic, upbeat, and practical guide full of ideas that will help young grads navigate the situation."

—David Vranicar, author of *The Lost Graduation: Stepping off Campus and Into a Crisis*

"Bonnie Snyder gives encouragement and strategic advice to college graduates who are navigating today's challenging job market, beginning with the importance of maintaining a patient, positive attitude. She is right on target when she says that career success may look bleak in the short term, but as older workers retire the long-term prospects for this generation are unlimited. By tapping into the inner and outer resources she discusses in her easy-to-read book, today's graduate will get the most from an often painful journey to enjoyable, full-time work."

—Nancy Anderson, career counselor and author of *Work with Passion: How to Do What You Love for a Living*

"In an arena of so much misinformation and uncertainty, Bonnie Snyder offers practical and valuable advice to American college graduates, from looking for a job to dealing with their student loans."

—Serge Bakalian and Aurora Meneghello, filmmakers of *Default: The Student Loan Documentary*

The Unemployed College Graduate's SURVIVAL GUIDE

The Unemployed College Graduate's SURVIVAL GUIDE

Bonnie Kerrigan Snyder, DEd, CCPS, Author of *The New College Reality*

How to Get Your Life Together, Deal with Debt, and Find a Job After College

Aadamsmedia

Avon, Massachusetts

Published by
Adams Media, a division of F+W Media, Inc.
57 Littlefield Street, Avon, MA 02322. U.S.A.
www.adamsmedia.com

ISBN 10: 1-4405-6023-4
ISBN 13: 978-1-4405-6023-1
eISBN 10: 1-4405-6024-2
eISBN 13: 978-1-4405-6024-8

Printed in the United States of America.

10   9   8   7   6   5   4   3   2   1

This publication is designed to provide accurate and authoritative information with regard to the subject matter covered. It is sold with the understanding that the publisher is not engaged in rendering legal, accounting, or other professional advice. If legal advice or other expert assistance is required, the services of a competent professional person should be sought.

—From a *Declaration of Principles* jointly adopted by
a Committee of the American Bar Association
and a Committee of Publishers and Associations

Many of the designations used by manufacturers and sellers to distinguish their product are claimed as trademarks. Where those designations appear in this book and F+W Media was aware of a trademark claim, the designations have been printed with initial capital letters.

This book is available at quantity discounts for bulk purchases.
For information, please call 1-800-289-0963.

"The hardest work in the world
is being out of work."

—Whitney Young

This book is dedicated to everyone who has ever faced unemployment or underemployment.

ACKNOWLEDGMENTS

I am grateful to my agent Miriam Altshuler, my editor Peter Archer, and everyone at F+W Media for believing in this book and bringing it to readers. Thanks also to family, friends, acquaintances, and even strangers for reaching out and sharing your personal stories of perseverance and your helpful strategies for finding and landing first jobs.

CONTENTS

INTRODUCTION

You did everything you thought you were supposed to do. You followed the rules, studied hard, and invested in a college education. You struggled and sacrificed until you finally had your chance to walk across the stage and collect your diploma. You expected all this hard work to pay off in numerous job offers, but so far—in terms of a job— what do you have to show for it?

I probably don't need to tell you that since 2008 the world economy has changed dramatically. Today's college graduates are facing the toughest employment market in decades. Instead of being greeted by eager employers welcoming you with open arms, you are facing stubbornly high unemployment levels, rising unrest among the young worldwide, and dire economic news. There is a famous Chinese saying that goes: May you live in interesting times. If this is something to be desired, then congratulations— you are living through some very interesting times, indeed!

It's easy to get discouraged when facing such daunting employment odds. But although you might want to blow off steam (understandably!) and this may even make you feel better temporarily, your primary challenge remains: You still need to find a way to support yourself.

Other books written for newly graduated college students give you solid advice on how to write a compelling resume, give a good interview, and conduct a thorough job hunt. This isn't one of those books (although we'll touch on some of these issues). Those books are for ordinary times, when there are reasonable numbers of job openings and an economy prepared to absorb new entrants. This is a book for extraordinary times, when the economy is down and job hunting is tough. This is a book about surviving when nothing seems fair.

Read this book and you'll be more ready to face today's world. You'll learn:

- **The basic facts about today's economy and the outlook for tomorrow**

- **How to deal with your student loans, with health insurance, and with finding a place to live**

- **How to build a new relationship with your parents, which may include living with them for a while**

- **What to do to generate income streams**

- **The value of networking—whether it's with family and friends, college acquaintances, or others**

Finally, you'll come to appreciate the importance of looking at things realistically and evaluating when and where you can find permanent employment.

Despite the bad economic news, there are plenty of reasons to feel hopeful about your future. Yes, the short-term employment forecast is rather gray and stormy, but the long-term economic forecast is actually quite bright for your generation. Believe it or not, the demographic tides will soon be turning in your favor, creating a likely labor shortage, and then the employment market should burst wide open. Meanwhile, you need a good short-term plan for how to survive the current economic downturn, as well as a long-range plan preparing yourself to take full advantage of future opportunities.

Your generation's path to economic security is going to look different than the one followed by earlier generations, but that doesn't mean that your journey will be any less enriching or exciting. There are opportunities to achieve success for every generation, in good times and in bad.

This book deals with both the mindset you need to beat the bleak employment odds and the practical and proactive strategies for finding immediate employment options and for locating resources to inform and guide you along the way. No one enjoys being unemployed, but it is also not the end of the world. With determination, persistence, a willingness to start at the bottom, and some hard-core budgeting skills, you will overcome this temporary setback and go far in spite of it. It's going to take some work on your part, however, so let's get started.

PART I

SURVIVAL

We all need to survive. At a bare minimum, you need to have a roof over your head, clothes on your back, food to eat, and access to medical care when you are sick. These are the basics. Unfortunately, supplying these fundamental needs costs money, and money seems to be in short supply these days.

It would be nice if colleges taught courses on how to make a living, but most do not. After graduation, you are congratulated on your academic accomplishments and sent off to seek your fortune in the workforce without a roadmap or a compass. It seems that alumni are supposed to somehow magically intuit the path to success all on their own. Oddly, it's always been this way. Back in the 1950s, the American satirist Tom Lehrer composed a humorous ditty about the difficult transition from school to work called "Bright College Days," which includes the unforgettable lines:

"Soon we'll be out amid the cold world's strife,
Soon we'll be sliding down the razor blade of life!"

If you feel like you're being sliced in half by a cruel, unforgiving labor market, you're not the first and you're not alone. Welcome to the jarring reality of adult life.

CHAPTER ONE

EMOTIONAL SURVIVAL

Graduating from college is a big rite of passage. You have completed one very long and arduous ordeal and you are looking forward to beginning your adult life. You're ready to move into a place of your own, start your first full-time job, and begin paying your own bills. After all, this is what people told you would happen. Your parents have probably already repainted your bedroom and turned it into a sewing room or a workout room. Let's face it—they're ready for you to be out on your own, and so are you.

As it turns out, though, reality doesn't follow the plan. Days stretch into weeks and weeks into months, and you still don't have a job. You feel bitter and disappointed. You might even feel angry or scared. Being unemployed can challenge your self-esteem, your dignity, and your sense of self-worth. Beyond that, it can also really challenge your ability to pay your bills! Inevitably, you start looking for someone or something to blame for your predicament.

IT'S NOT YOUR FAULT!

First of all, don't blame yourself. You didn't do anything wrong. It's normal to feel shell-shocked and temporarily overwhelmed as a new college graduate even in a *good* economy. After all, you're suddenly cut loose from a familiar education system that nurtured you most of your life, and then expected to find your way in a new arena you barely understand. In a bad economy, though, the transition from student to worker is going to be even harder, so you're going to have to be extra patient and go easy on yourself. It won't do any good to beat yourself up while you're having trouble finding work, and it would be pretty counterproductive.

BY THE NUMBERS

It's a tough time for college graduates seeking entry-level employment in many parts of the world. The former British prime minister, Gordon Brown, has warned of a global youth unemployment epidemic, with 81 million people under the age of twenty-five currently without work. According to *Education News,* between 2002 and 2007 the hourly wage for college grads fell nearly 5 percent while the cost of living increased 18.5 percent. Even more astonishingly, 45 percent of college graduates who are able to find work are earning less than $15,000 annually two years after graduation!

Here in the United States, more than two million college graduates are now unemployed and millions more are currently underemployed. Young adults are unemployed at nearly double the rate of older Americans, and their incomes have declined much faster than that of the national average. According to the U.S. Bureau of Labor Statistics, the jobless rate for younger workers with a college degree has more than doubled since the financial crisis began. The average length of unemployment is now more than forty weeks, higher than it was even during the Great Depression. A recent government report on "Unemployment Among Young Workers" shows that one in five young workers is unemployed—the highest rate of unemployment ever recorded for this age group. Also, young workers make up a disproportionate share of those without jobs. They comprise just 13 percent of the labor force, but a hefty 26 percent of the unemployed.

If you're under the age of twenty-five, you may have particular difficulty finding steady, high-quality work. About half of the workers in this age group are currently "underutilized," meaning they're either unemployed or working part-time, below their capabilities, outside of the college labor market, such as in restaurant or retail work.

Your situation isn't helped by the fact that you've just left a highly structured environment—college—for the unstructured world of job searching. It's a bit like leaving a swimming pool to dive into the ocean. The swimming skills you've learned are going to be essential to surviving, but it's a bit overwhelming at first.

No matter how much you read and hear about the broader trends of youth unemployment, let's face it: You're primarily interested in your own specific job situation and what to do about it. That's not only understandable, but it's also the right attitude to have. You have to be concerned with your own well-being at this point! You're facing a big challenge that demands your full attention. But—and this is an essential point to remember—*it is not insurmountable.*

PLACING YOUR PROBLEM IN PERSPECTIVE

Before we address your individual concerns, let's take a step back and look at the broader economic picture. Viewing your personal dilemma from a wider perspective can help you understand the scope of what you are dealing with in order to formulate a more effective response.

If you don't look at things from the macro-level—that is, the "big picture"—it is easy to think that the world is an unpredictable place and that nothing you do will make any difference. But the first step in getting a grip on your problem is understanding its roots. For that you need an expanded viewpoint. When you recognize the larger forces at play, you can begin to access information that can help you form reliable predictions and make intelligent plans for confronting a changing reality. This allows you to regain control over your choices, your plans, and your destiny—and that's empowering.

There are many forces at play contributing to your difficulty finding the kind of work you want.

- ■ *Globalization* has shifted many manufacturing jobs to countries with lower wages.

- ■ *Outsourcing* has done the same with many digital jobs.

- ■ *Technology* has eliminated certain easy-to-automate positions.

- ■ *Debt crisis* has plagued many economies, especially those in Europe.

- ■ *Financial meltdown* in 2008 following the housing crash created a worldwide crisis that many are now dubbing "The Great Recession."

All of these are factors in slowing the entire economy. And none of them is your fault.

Part of the problem is demographic. The wheels driving the current economic squeeze were set in motion more than a half century ago with the arrival of the oversized Baby

Boomer generation. That group is now reaching retirement age, but is reluctant to retire, holding on to jobs that might, under other circumstances, have gone to younger workers. These are large, powerful forces beyond your control, which nevertheless affect your current predicament.

It Won't Last Forever

You didn't create this problem, but you're going to have to deal with it. And you will. There is even good demographic news on the horizon for you, which I will discuss in Chapter 7, so remember that sometimes these dramatic, historic shifts can work in your favor. Keep that in mind as you plan your strategy and scan the economic horizon for upcoming opportunities.

The poor employment market is bad luck for you, but it need not be ruinous. It is merely unfortunate, but it is most definitely not the end of the world or an indication of your long-term prospects in life. Think of it as the opening chapter of a wonderful triumphing-over-adversity story.

Being unemployed is also not a measure of your worth or value as a person. This is a temporary situation and you will eventually rise above it. It is merely a rough patch in a long career road that will have many ups and downs.

The good news is, you're not alone. You are not the only one going through this struggle, and millions of other college graduates know exactly how you feel.

With unemployment high, employers can be very choosy. It's a buyer's market and employers are calling the shots. It won't always be this way, of course, but for now many potential employers are waiting to see whether the economy turns around before adding more people to their payroll. If you're a brand-new college graduate, you also have to compete with last year's unemployed graduates, many of whom are still looking for jobs.

═════════BY THE NUMBERS═════════

According to the Bureau of Labor Statistics, there are currently more than 482,000 customer service representatives with college degrees, along with 317,000 waiters and waitresses. There are also more than 80,000 bartenders and 18,000 parking lot attendants—a total of 17 million Americans with college degrees working at jobs that do not require college-level skills. Currently, there is a surplus of applicants (estimates are four to five) for every available position.

═════════════════$═════════════════

Obviously, right now you are facing some stiff odds, especially when you consider that unemployed graduates don't even show up in official unemployment statistics. That's because in order to count as unemployed, first you have to have a job!

If you've had to move back home with your family after college to live more affordably, you also have plenty of company besides your new living companions. Analysts now estimate that between 80 and 85 percent of new college graduates will return home to live after graduation due to their inability to find a job offering sufficient pay to live independently. According to the Pew Research Center, there are now more multigenerational U.S. households than at almost any point in modern history—a record 49 million Americans live with members of an older or a younger generation, the highest percentage since the 1950s. Still, knowing that other college graduates are also struggling to move out doesn't make your personal situation any easier for you to tolerate.

Now, I know I've been piling it on a bit heavily, and you may be thinking you couldn't possibly have worse luck. Each generation is supposed to do better than their parents, and it looks like yours may be the first generation to be moving backward economically. Before you jump to any conclusions, however, I want you to take a longer view of history. It's true that your generation is currently facing some very bad economic news. Your generation is not, however, the first generation of young people to have to overcome difficult times.

REMEMBER THE GREAT DEPRESSION

Consider the harsh circumstances young adults faced during the Great Depression. During that era, my grandfather saved up enough money to go to college by working as a ranch hand, only to lose it all when the bank where he kept his account failed. (This was before the FDIC insured bank deposits.) Back in the 1930s, only a very small proportion of young people could afford to attend college at all; putting food on the table and keeping a roof over their heads took a much higher priority. Many members of the World War II generation missed college altogether or were pulled from school when they were drafted and sent abroad to risk their lives fighting a European war. Some never returned. The Korean War and, more recently, the Vietnam War also disrupted and cut short many young lives. Young men not even old enough to vote were given no choice about the dangerous path their lives would suddenly take.

More recently, Generation X faced challenges similar to yours in finding suitable employment during the deep economic recession of the 1980s. When I graduated from college during those years, we were the first generation to follow the numerous Baby Boomers. It was tough to find work. The Boomers had gotten there first, had more work experience than we did, and were hardly in short supply.

Generation X even coined the word "McJobs" to describe their dim employment prospects and the demeaning jobs many were forced to accept. Many members of this generation responded to the unwelcoming workforce by becoming independently entrepreneurial and charting creative new paths. As a result, they were instrumental in creating the Internet and the information revolution, the effects of which continue to influence our world. So, sometimes a seemingly unfortunate event can turn out to be the best thing that could have happened.

These prior generations didn't anticipate having their educations and careers unexpectedly interrupted by worldwide events or economic calamities, but that's what happened to them. I'm pretty sure they weren't too happy about it at the time, but they couldn't foresee what the future would bring. So, while the employment situation for today's college graduates is certainly disheartening, it's important not to overindulge in self-pity or defeatism. Where would we be today if these prior generations had given up? Instead, they faced their unique challenges with fortitude and made the best of their existing opportunities. You will, too. You will rise to this challenge and chart an entirely new and exciting path that will mark your generation as creative and innovative survivors.

As best you can, try to accept your circumstances with optimism, a broad view, and a philosophical outlook. The attitude with which you face this early career disappointment will determine whether you emerge from your current trials with your courage and enthusiasm intact, or whether you will be permanently damaged and impoverished by the ordeal. Rest assured that you can and will overcome your present challenges and become a better, significantly wiser person for having done so. You may even learn something meaningful from this experience that will pay off for you down the line.

A sense of humor can help a lot, too. For instance, comedian Conan O'Brien recently delivered a rousing commencement speech to Dartmouth graduates in which he acknowledged their bumpy entrance to employment. It's a great speech, and I encourage you to watch it in its entirety on YouTube. O'Brien offered graduates helpful advice, such as: "If you live on ramen noodles for too long, you lose all

feelings in your hands and your stool becomes a white gel."
He told parents: "You will spend more money framing your child's diploma than they will earn in the next six months. It's tough out there, so be patient. The only people hiring right now are Panera Bread and Mexican drug cartels."

Then he shifted to some personal thoughts on the importance of facing career disappointment without giving up. Here, he spoke from personal experience as the recently fired host of *The Tonight Show*:

> Nietzsche famously said, "Whatever doesn't kill you makes you stronger." But what he failed to stress is that it almost kills you. Disappointment stings, and for driven, successful people like yourselves it is disorienting. What Nietzsche should have said is "Whatever doesn't kill you, makes you watch a lot of Cartoon Network and drink midprice Chardonnay at 11 in the morning."
>
> Now, by definition, commencement speakers at an Ivy League college are considered successful. But a little over a year ago, I experienced a profound and very public disappointment. I did not get what I wanted, and I left a system that had nurtured and helped define me for the better part of seventeen years. . . .
>
> But then something spectacular happened. Fogbound, with no compass, and adrift, I started trying things. I grew a strange, cinnamon beard. I dove into the world of social media. I started tweeting my comedy. I threw

together a national tour. I played the guitar. I did stand-up, wore a skin-tight blue leather suit, recorded an album, made a documentary, and frightened my friends and family.

Ultimately, I abandoned all preconceived perceptions of my career path and stature . . . I did a lot of silly, unconventional, spontaneous, and seemingly irrational things and guess what: with the exception of the blue leather suit, it was the most satisfying and fascinating year of my professional life. To this day I still don't understand exactly what happened, but I have never had more fun, been more challenged—and this is important—had more conviction about what I was doing. How could this be true? Well, it's simple: There are few things more liberating in this life than having your worst fear realized.

If O'Brien is right, consider yourself already liberated! Facing unemployment at the outset of your career may inoculate you against the terror and powerlessness many on the traditional career path feel over the prospect of losing a seemingly secure job. It may require you to be more flexible and open to numerous possible ways of making a living, such as striking out overseas, starting your own business, partnering with family or friends, or pursuing independent freelancing opportunities. In short, it may force you to remove your blinders and consider the full range of ways to support yourself while finding greater ultimate fulfillment in your life.

BY THE NUMBERS

Bear in mind that as bad as things are in the United States, there are many other countries where the situation is far worse. According to a *Wall Street Journal* article titled "Generation Jobless," while U.S. workers between ages fifteen and twenty-four had an unemployment rate of 18.4 percent last year, that is still considerably lower than the European Union's rate of 20 percent. In Greece, 32.9 percent of young people are unemployed, while in Spain the figure has now topped an astonishing 50 percent! Clearly, your employment prospects are better than in many other parts of the world.

REACH OUT FOR EMOTIONAL SUPPORT

Sometimes, it's not enough to receive encouragement or to be reminded that there are reasons to be optimistic. You may need additional help. Please reach out for emotional support if you are so overwhelmed by your current difficulties that you feel you cannot cope. I hope that you understand that it is not your fault if you are unemployed, but you may need extra assistance if you are struggling with deep, lasting feelings of sadness, anger, or other emotional pain that you just can't shake; having suicidal thoughts; or cannot provide for your basic needs. Tragically, some unemployed graduates have resorted to suicide, and the Centers for Disease Control recently found, in a long-term study, that suicide rates tend to rise when the economy declines. Unemployment is a big emotional challenge that presents practical day-to-day problems, and there is absolutely no shame in asking for help when you need it. Quite the opposite.

Seek Out Counselors

I hope you have supportive friends and family who understand what you are going through and who try to help you, but sometimes that kind of help isn't available or it isn't enough. You should know that there is also professional help available to you, regardless of your economic circumstances. Every town has counseling centers, most of which offer reduced fees or free services to clients who do not have insurance or cannot afford to pay the full price. A simple phonebook or Google search of "Counseling" will produce a list of appropriate agencies in your immediate area. You will probably want to search for counselors rather than psychiatrists or psychologists. Counselors specialize in helping ordinary people who are going through temporary life difficulties, whereas psychologists and psychiatrists tend to specialize in working with people with diagnosable problems. Counselors also tend to charge a bit less than psychiatrists and psychologists.

Your college's counseling center may be able to refer you to available resources, so you could contact them to ask for their advice on where to turn for assistance. Many churches and other religious organizations also offer low-cost or free counseling services to people in the community. Do not be afraid to take advantage of these services, which are there precisely to support you when you need help. Job centers are another community resource that may be able to provide some basic counseling and referral services, so if you are receiving assistance there, ask them about how to access other support services. You can find information on job centers in the recommended resources at the end of the book.

You can find a comprehensive list of therapists in the United States and Canada online at *www.therapists. psychologytoday.com*. This resource includes a description of their services and therapeutic approach. It might make sense to seek a therapist with capabilities in career counseling, along with any other support services you may be seeking. Also, at any time—twenty-four hours a day seven days a week—you can reach out to the National Suicide Prevention Hotline toll-free at 1-800-273-TALK (8255). If you are ever feeling desperate, please pick up the phone.

Take advantage of any emotional support resources available to you and ask for help paying for it when necessary. You deserve emotional support during this trying time and should not hesitate to seek appropriate assistance, to which you are entitled.

UNPRODUCTIVE EMOTIONS AREN'T WORTH INDULGING

When unfortunate things happen, it is natural to have a negative emotional response. You're only human, after all.

Sending out resumes and receiving only rejections or, even more annoying, no response at all, can lead to some pretty pessimistic thinking. When we experience any sort of injury, it is common to want to retreat while we recover. While it is completely understandable to want to spend some time licking your wounds and examining your grievances, this can become unproductive and start to interfere with your ability to make progress if you engage in these activities for too long. Following are a few attitudes that are not going to help you move forward.

═══════BY THE NUMBERS═══════

While the official overall unemployment rate has been hovering above 8 percent, the jobless rate for college graduates twenty-five years and older is just 4.5 percent. Young adults twenty to twenty-four years old with only a high school diploma face a high unemployment rate of nearly 20 percent, but numerous studies have confirmed that college graduates in this age group have lower unemployment rates (around 8 percent) than those without the degree (33 percent for those without a high school diploma). Unemployment rates for high school graduates and dropouts remain much higher than for those of college graduates; according to the U.S. Congress Joint Economic Committee, earning a four-year college degree reduced the probability of being unemployed to one in twelve.

$=============\text{\$}=============$

But It's Not Fair!

Maybe it isn't fair that you graduated into a major recession, but this kind of thinking won't get you anywhere. Don't get stuck on the fairness issue. *Life is not fair*: there— I said it. Part of adulthood is grasping that reality.

There will always be people better and worse off than you. It's up to you to successfully play the hand that life has dealt you. The sooner you accept that life is not fair and resolve to improve your circumstances in spite of that immutable fact, the sooner you will be able to advance productively. The longer you entertain that pointless line of thinking, the longer you will remained mired in negativity and wheel-spinning.

Also, be aware that just because you went to college, or assumed a large student debt load, doesn't obligate a potential employer to care. Like every individual party in an economic transaction, employers are self-interested. The only reason they will make you a job offer is if they have reason to expect that hiring you will provide a net economic gain to their organization. They really couldn't care less about how hard you worked in school or how much money you owe to your creditors; all they care about is what you can do for them right now.

I *Need* What I'm Asking For

Allow me to make a quick comparison to the housing market. If you paid a high price for a house, and then housing prices drop, no one is obligated to pay you more for your house than the market currently dictates. The next buyer isn't interested in how much you owe on your mortgage or how much you think your house "should" be worth, and this information will not influence how much he or she is willing to pay for it.

I once had a rather frustrating conversation with a relative who had a home for sale. He had received an offer close to his original asking price but rejected it, saying: "I *need* to get $280,000 for this house and I'm not accepting anything less. I owe a lot on the mortgage and then I also have credit card debts to repay." He was hoping to make a tidy profit on the sale, and wanted to hold out for more. I knew that the market was sinking fast and suggested that he reconsider the offer. I pointed out that the next buyer wouldn't care how much money my relative thought he ought to receive for the house; the buyer would only be interested in getting the best deal on the house that he could. My advice was waved away. Ultimately, the house sold for far less than the original offer, as the market sank like a stone while the seller unsuccessfully held out for the amount of money he thought he deserved.

The truth is, a house is only "worth" what someone is willing to pay for it now, regardless of how much you paid for it when you bought it or how much money you might wish to receive. As the great English writer Aldous Huxley put it, "Facts do not cease to exist because they are ignored." When I was a child, a science teacher once explained to me that denying that natural laws exist doesn't suspend their effect. You can deny the law of gravity, but if you jump off the edge of the Grand Canyon you will soon discover that your personal opinions on the matter are irrelevant.

The point is, the market determines what labor is worth and which jobs and applicants are in high demand. Denying this reality doesn't exempt you from being subject to it. There is no point in being upset or offended by it; it makes far more sense to adapt to the rules of the prevailing labor market in order to find success in it.

My College Education Wasn't Worth It

As an unemployed college graduate, you may be struggling with regrets or feeling like your college degree was not worth the effort, particularly if you have hefty student loans to repay. Don't think that way! College education remains a worthwhile endeavor with inherent value. Don't play the blame game. Colleges don't promise jobs; they promise you a college education. That is what you paid for and that is what you received, and it is enriching in ways that can't be measured in mere money. It was a fair exchange, and no one can ever take that achievement, or the learning that went along with it, away from you.

Finding a job is a different matter entirely. It is a fresh start, and the critical thinking skills you gained in college can assist you in analyzing the job market and making intelligent choices moving forward. Your college education was an entirely separate activity from your need to get a job now. Now you must use that education, and your problem-solving abilities, to figure out how to make a living, given the current market conditions.

Even in underemployment situations, where a college graduate takes a position below the college level, as is occurring throughout the workforce right now, the person with the degree is likely to win a position over a less-educated individual. In other words, you might not be thrilled to be working at Starbucks, but it's better than having no job at all! As you can see from the following chart, while the unemployment rates for young workers have increased overall, college graduates continue to have the lowest levels.

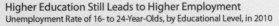

Higher Education Still Leads to Higher Employment
Unemployment Rate of 16- to 24-Year-Olds, by Educational Level, in 2010

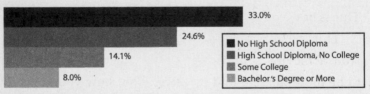

33.0%
24.6%
14.1%
8.0%

■ No High School Diploma
■ High School Diploma, No College
■ Some College
■ Bachelor's Degree or More

Source: *Unemployment Among Young Workers Report*, Bureau of Labor Statistics

Rest assured that your college degree was not a mistake. Just because the economy is bad doesn't mean that your education wasn't "worth it" or that it will not "pay off" in the long run. You have acquired knowledge that you will be able to put to use in all aspects of your life, and you should not regret your decision to pursue higher education. It has value and worth apart from its marketability in the workforce.

That being said, don't assume that just because you graduated from college that you are done preparing yourself for a job. Be willing to do whatever it takes to succeed in this economy, even if it means pursuing additional training, licensure, certification, or other academic credentials. The college degree can be considered foundational to the career or professional training you might need to pursue to find your place in the evolving economy.

WHAT IS GOING TO HELP

Your best allies in this tough battle to support yourself are going to be your positive mental attitude and your willingness to do whatever it takes to get where you want to go. This is how you will beat today's tough employment odds.

This economic recession does not have to stop you from achieving your career goals. However, you may have to be more flexible and creative about how you arrive at your destination. Sometimes, you need to alter your route when you find one road is blocked. Other generations before you have also faced hard times and unfair circumstances. Many charted their own paths, and some of them went on to start successful start-up companies, because they found traditional avenues of advancement closed to them. You can, too.

In their book *The Start-Up of You*, LinkedIn founder Reid Hoffman and Ben Casnocha argue that you need to think about your career launch as an entrepreneurial venture. They point out that the traditional career "escalator" of entry and advancement is jammed, because the older generation refuses to step off at the top and the competition for opportunity is fierce. This requires fresh thinking and different strategies from what worked in the past.

You're going to have to take this setback in stride and not let it disrupt your long-term career goals. You must start with what is possible, no matter how humble, and work yourself up from there. Tennis great Arthur Ashe advised: "Start where you are. Use what you have. Do what you can." This is great advice for those struggling to make a first career step. You must begin with the resources and opportunities available to you at this moment; that is all anyone can do, and that is enough.

The economy won't always be bad, but the ingenuity and persistence that you learn now, in overcoming these hurdles, will likely prove invaluable to you for the rest of your career. Your early career may not follow the route you expected, but you may find unexpected joys and rewards if you open yourself to the possibilities and carve out new opportunities for yourself.

In fact, early indications seem to show that this generation of graduates, having different life experiences than their predecessors, may adopt different values, as well. For instance, polls conducted by Harvard's Institute of Politics indicate that members of the current "Millennial" generation (between ages sixteen and twenty-four) are less focused on seeking fortune and fame. Instead, their hopes for the future center on making a contribution to society and maintaining a close network of personal contacts. This is heartening news and may lead to a more meaningful and fulfilling life path than what was pursued by your more materialistic predecessors.

There are still going to be opportunities to find good jobs in the economy, but the openings are shifting and you can't look in the rearview mirror at where the jobs used to be. Instead, you have to look ahead to where the jobs are heading. You must be smart and learn to read the economic indicators to distinguish which way the winds are blowing. You graduated from college, so you have already demonstrated that you have perseverance and that you can process huge amounts of information, learn from it, and draw solid conclusions. Now, let's apply those skills to your own employment problem and figure out the best solutions to your problem.

CHAPTER TWO

ECONOMIC SURVIVAL

I want you to take a deep breath. You're probably feeling like you are under a lot of pressure right now, so I want you to inhale deeply, hold it for a second, and then let it all out. Try to relax. Everything will work out much better if you stay calm and focus on what you can do—right here and right now—to make the best of your current situation.

Okay, so you've already figured out that your first job hunt is not going to be a stroll in the park, a piece of cake, or a Sunday picnic. You understand the odds you're facing and you've resolved to do whatever it takes to support yourself and get a shaky toehold on the career ladder. I commend you for your mental toughness and your determination to get up and get moving.

As an unemployed college graduate, you undoubtedly have bills to pay. You need to eat and you need to keep a roof over your head. You may also have student loans to repay. We'll be talking about how to manage those a little bit later. You probably want to start living on your own, but you may feel unable to afford moving out of your parents' house yet. You don't have to figure out all the answers right now. But you do have to survive. So, let's talk about how you're going to do that.

STAY AFLOAT!

The first thing you need to do is figure out how to earn some money fast doing whatever it takes until you can find a job worthy of your abilities. There is absolutely no shame in this, even though it may require you to swallow some of your pride and adjust some of your expectations. In fact, there is a great deal of dignity in always making the best of your circumstances, no matter how difficult they may be at the moment.

I like to make a distinction between what I call "staying afloat" and "getting to shore." If you were knocked off a boat at sea with no life vest, your first mission would be to keep your head above water and stay afloat. This survival necessity takes priority over everything else, and you will desperately tread water with everything you've got to make sure you don't sink below the waves!

Once you have managed to stay afloat, and you are confident that drowning is not imminent, you can begin to breathe more calmly and survey your situation a bit more broadly. You will look off in the distance to see if you can spot any secure locations where you could improve your current predicament and reach safety. If you spot a boat—or better yet, land—you will turn in that direction and start heading that way. Your ultimate goal, of course, is "getting to shore." Once you're safely ashore, you can collect your wits and begin figuring out how to make the most of your new, improved situation.

As an unemployed college graduate, with bills to pay but no job, you are struggling to stay afloat financially. Your ultimate goal is obviously going to be to get to shore— meaning in a permanent career position with benefits and hopefully upward mobility. But first you have to deal with your current crisis situation. You need a short-term plan to survive before you can implement your long-term plan for how you are going to thrive.

To better understand this, let's turn to an idea called Maslow's "hierarchy of needs." The developmental psychologist Abraham Maslow believed that we all have lower-order needs that have to be met before we can focus on higher, more idealistic aspirations. At the most basic level, we all need to survive. We require food, water, and shelter. In the modern world, these necessities cost money. Once these fundamental needs are met, we can begin focusing on our "higher" needs, such as finding an occupation that is enriching and satisfying and that allows us to utilize and develop our full talents.

I believe the phrase "any port in a storm" applies here, as well. A ship at sea may be heading for a certain port of call, but if an unexpected hurricane suddenly threatens the survival of the entire crew, then the captain will wisely order them to seek safety at the nearest available harbor, regardless of how desirable that location may be. The crew are not going to be choosy about where they find emergency shelter until the storm passes. They will worry about getting to their final destination later.

The same principle can help you to navigate today's treacherous employment waters, until you can reach your final career destination. By this, I mean that you may need to seek temporary shelter in any available position while still pursuing your ultimate career goals. Your long-term goals and aspirations do not have to change, but your short-term behavior may have to adapt to the current circumstances.

BY THE NUMBERS

Rutgers University conducted a survey of recent college graduates and found that many of them are making significant concessions in their first jobs. For instance, 27 percent described their first job as "just a job to get you by" while 46 percent described it as "a steppingstone to a career," rather than a career. Thirty-nine percent accepted "a lot less" in salary than they had anticipated. So, if you are thinking that you didn't get the employment deal you were hoping to get, obviously you have a lot of company. Furthermore, 33 percent are working below the level of their education, 23 percent work outside their interest area, 23 percent took a job without health benefits, 21 percent work unfavorable hours, and 13 percent only have a temporary job. These numbers are all higher than previous reports from earlier college graduates.

$

As a college graduate, you probably never expected to find yourself working in a coffeehouse, bartending, or manning a call center, but if you do, rest assured that you are not alone and that this is not a disgraceful outcome or a permanent condition. The *New York Times* published an article called "Generation Limbo" in which it details the stories of several graduates, some Ivy League, who are working stop-gap jobs to make ends meet while still seeking better opportunities. If they can do it, so can you.

No, working a menial job to make "staying afloat" money may not be ideal, but there is the satisfaction that comes from paying your own bills and there is nothing demeaning about an honest day's work in any occupation. Instead, you should be proud of facing a challenging circumstance head-on and persevering despite difficult odds. You don't need to give up on your long-term goal of finding a more suitable career, but, for now, any job that helps you keep your financial head above water is worthwhile. Financial survival is priority number one! Once you have accomplished that, you can begin thinking about maximizing your career potential.

At this point, I am going to assume that you have already sent your well-written resume around to all of your preferred employers and come up empty. (There are plenty of books on the market about how to write a compelling resume. For an excellent guide and samples, see Martin Yate's *Knock 'em Dead Resumes*.) You have bills and loans to pay and you're starting to get pretty anxious, if not downright desperate. Let's talk about some of the possible options available to you to start making money right away so that you have enough cash in your checking account to pay them. I am going to divide these options into "College-Level Emergency Work" and "Sub-College-Level Emergency Work."

COLLEGE-LEVEL EMERGENCY WORK

Temporary Agencies

A temporary agency is a firm that supplies employers with qualified workers on an as-needed basis. Some well-known temporary agencies are Manpower, Kelly Services, and Spherion. To locate more, simply go to the Yellow Pages or run a Google search of "temporary agencies" or "employment agencies" in your local area. Temporary agencies tend to be plentiful in major cities, but even small towns and suburbs have them.

If you need to find work, visit your local temporary agencies and register with them as soon as possible. These agencies will be very interested in determining the job skills that you possess, and they may test you to measure your proficiency with typing, computation, or computer skills and software capabilities. Local businesses in sudden need of replacement help will often contact these agencies on short notice, and you want to be sure that you are already in line when work appears. Employers like to use temp agencies because they prescreen workers to certify that they can handle the assigned work. This saves companies a lot of time.

Temp agencies can also be great sources of information about which local firms are hiring and what types of skills are currently in high demand and short supply. For instance, some temp agencies specialize in certain types of work roles that are hard to find, such as accounting services or health care. If you are unclear about your career direction, or considering further training, you should pay very close attention to which fields are currently in such need of workers that they will pay a premium to hire temp workers and consider pursuing any necessary credentials in those areas. Consider it an applied, graduate-level research project. Also, notice which fields pay most highly and ask yourself whether you would be suited to train for those careers. You might discover a possible career path this way.

Temp to Permanent

Although temporary workers typically do not receive benefits, temp work often has a way of turning into a permanent job, much like a paid internship. A survey by Manpower found that 30 percent of their recent temporary placements turned into full-time positions within a year. So, you should view each temporary assignment as a job interview. If you work hard and impress your supervisor with your results on a temporary assignment, it is possible that he or she will try to find a way to keep you on, full-time. At the very least, he should be willing to write you a nice recommendation letter or to refer you to colleagues in other firms. Temp work is also a way of adding respectable, career-level experience and references to your resume, so this should be one of your first stops when searching for emergency work.

Tutoring

As a recent college graduate, you are probably very well informed and up-to-date in your subject area. If you studied an academic discipline such as math, science, or English, then you may be able to earn decent money tutoring younger students who are struggling in these required subjects in high school or middle school.

To find work as a tutor, you should contact the local school districts in your area and ask them if they keep a list of tutors to recommend to inquiring students and their families. You may even be allowed to hang flyers advertising your services in the guidance office or to drop off business cards. Be sure to let the special education teachers in the school know that you are available for tutoring, also.

Don't forget to contact local private schools, as well. Some private schools may even allow you to come in during the school day and work with students during their study halls. I know two private tutors working at a private school who are there full-time, earning between $40 and $50 an hour for their time. They are so busy that they are turning away clients. There are even some specialized tutors charging up to $100 an hour for their services!

Public schools have certification requirements, so you will probably not be allowed to work with students during the school day in those venues, but they may allow you to meet with students in classrooms after school. Otherwise, you will probably have to make arrangements to meet with students at their homes or in a public library.

Help with Test Preparation

If you had high SAT, ACT, or AP test scores, you may be able to make money by helping students prepare for those standardized tests. Princeton Review and Kaplan are often looking for qualified instructors, and they offer training. These jobs tend to be high turnover, so they are almost always looking for new hires. You can go to their websites to learn about their recruiting procedures and eligibility requirements. (*www.princetonreview.com* and *www.kaptest.com*). However, if you are knowledgeable and informed, you may be able to offer individual test preparation services and keep all of your earnings yourself. There are even online sites where you can register and advertise your services as a tutor. Craigslist is one obvious site, and you should also check out WyzAnt.com, which specializes in matching tutors with clients.

Substitute Teaching

Whether or not you majored in education, you can become a substitute teacher with just a college degree in most parts of the country. Most school districts do not require a teaching certificate for substitutes, although they generally require a bachelor's degree. Depending on demand in your area, some districts may only require two years of college.

To become a substitute teacher, you will need to register with your local school district. Call the school districts in your immediate area to inquire about their policies and expectations for substitute teachers. There are also substitute teaching firms that service several districts, and you can register with them, as well. A simple Google search of "substitute teaching" should reveal these agencies if they exist in your area.

Substitute teachers are normally paid on a per-diem basis. Occasionally, you can find "long-term" substitute positions, such as when a teacher takes a maternity leave. These long-term positions are typically awarded to the most reliable substitute teachers.

The general rule with substitute teaching is that "the early bird gets the worm." In other words, when they call at 5 or 6 A.M. to offer you work, you'd better be prepared to say "Yes" and take the job that day. If you turn them down too many times, they will stop calling you and the assignments will go to someone else. The good news is, if you are reliable and willing to show up on time whenever and wherever you are needed, you will find yourself getting called more and more often. The pay for substitutes is not bad—generally somewhere between $70 and $100 a day, with higher rates in major cities.

There are also certain advantages to being a substitute teacher. One of the main ones is that the regular classroom teacher is supposed to provide you with the lesson plans and handle the grading of tests and assignments. Normally, you should not have to take work home with you, as the regular teacher would. However, the best substitutes will arrive prepared with back-up lesson plans in the event that the regular teacher fails to live up to these expectations.

Being extra prepared and willing to tackle additional duties is a great way to stand out as a substitute teacher. Another important attribute is the ability to handle disciplinary problems. Substitute teaching is also a great way for an unemployed teacher to make a favorable impression on administrators and to make connections that may lead to a permanent job offer. It may even convince some liberal arts graduates to earn their teaching credentials and pursue a career in education.

Freelancing

It's probably not fair to call freelancing "emergency" work, because this is a viable, long-term career option for many people who prefer to work flexibly and to call their own career shots. However, freelancing can also be a temporary money-earning alternative for people who would prefer to be hired in a full-time position.

As a college graduate, you have undoubtedly developed some advanced skills that have value in the marketplace. Thanks to the Internet, it is now relatively easy and inexpensive for you to advertise these services to an unlimited number of potential customers. With a simple PayPal account, you can even receive payments online.

Theoretically, you could be operating your freelance business from your local Starbucks, without incurring so much as an Internet connection as an expense (although you may be pushing your luck, as I've read that Starbucks is cracking down on so-called "squatters." But just the fact that Starbucks feels the need to do this shows you how common it is!) The point is that freelancing offers a relatively easy entry to the world of business entrepreneurship with a very low start-up cost.

There are even some well-established freelancing sites to help you get started, including *www.elance.com, www.guru.com,* and *www.freelancer.com.* If you're not sure what kind of services you could offer, try browsing these sites to see what sort of work is available. This is sure to stir your creative juices. There is work for content providers (that means writers), designers, artists, programmers, and many other creative specialties. You can post an online profile outlining your background and capabilities and showcasing your portfolio and begin bidding on open jobs very quickly.

While freelancing doesn't offer traditional job benefits, many find the lifestyle so appealing that they can't imagine working any other way. Furthermore, when you set up shop as a freelancer, you may be able to begin taking the many business deductions available to those working from a home office. This can include a portion of your rent and utilities, which are necessary for you to operate. Even if your home-based freelance business is not making a profit for a few years, those deductions can prove very valuable and can help you minimize your fixed monthly expenses. Be sure to keep receipts of all of your bills and expenditures throughout the year to take advantage of tax write-offs and to educate yourself on the rules and restrictions about taking them.

Discover the Pleasures and Advantages of "Coworking"

If you don't think you can afford to rent office space for your business idea, but you would rather not work from home, consider the new idea of "coworking" or "shared workspaces." This is an arrangement where several freelancers or entrepreneurs share a common office space and split the costs. It's a very intriguing business model and a much more affordable alternative than renting your own office space. Coworking offers several appealing advantages beyond the economical, such as companionship, mentorship, synergy, and the potential for collaboration.

A typical coworking site will have people working in several different fields, such as photography, writing, website design, marketing, or whatever other business you can imagine. Currently, coworking tends to be most popular with those under forty, so in these work arrangements you will find a younger mindset and youthful energy. A group environment with entrepreneurs in their twenties and early thirties is sure to produce plenty of creative ideas and enthusiasm, a very attractive aspect to working this way. A good coworking arrangement can help you develop more confidence and build business poise. You will be exposed, in close quarters, to many other people running successful businesses and can surely learn from their examples. Some coworking locations even attract the notice of employers searching for talented hires who are demonstrating initiative by getting started on their own in a creative endeavor. Being listed on a coworking site can help you gain exposure in your local business community. This can be much better for your career prospects and for your spirits than working from home, where no one sees you at all during the day.

Many large cities offer established coworking sites, and they are now springing up in smaller towns, too. A group of forward-thinking individuals in my small city on the East Coast recently converted an abandoned downtown candy factory into a coworking site; it was filled within a year and now they are expanding to accommodate their growing waiting list of people wishing to join. They named the site "The Candy Factory," and their motto is "Where working together is sweet!" You can read more about this site at *www.candyissweet.com.*

You can become a part-time coworker at this location for as little as $55 a month! This fee includes some space at a large working table, Internet access, a shared printer, and use of their business mailing address. For a higher fee, you can have your own desk. It is a downtown location, perfect for meeting with clients, and presents a professional, serious image. This coworking site also offers an attractive website advertising the services and products offered by each of its members. Cleverly, each business owner then becomes a potential source of referrals to their growing community. At most coworking sites, you don't have to sign a long-term lease, so it is very easy to try out this workstyle with little risk or investment.

Shared workspaces have become very popular in the San Francisco Bay Area with technology entrepreneurs, and they even attract venture capitalists searching for the next big idea. The Plug and Play Tech Center (*www.plugandplaytechcenter.com*) based in Sunnyvale, California, offers mentoring, networking opportunities, and hiring help to its members. They are planning expansion into Pittsburgh, Chicago, San Diego, Denver, and Vancouver. These modern twists on traditional working environments provide a dynamic habitat where cross-pollination of business ideas can easily occur.

Many shared workspaces place a welcome emphasis on educating their members. They offer organized workshops on topics of interest to start-up businesses, such as accounting, marketing, and incorporation. In this sense, it can become like a business incubator combined with continued learning. You may be able to find ideas for collaboration among the membership, while developing a more polished, professional identity for yourself.

To learn more about coworking opportunities, start with: *www.coworking.com* or Google "coworking" in your local area. You should also check out the coworking wiki page, *www.wiki.coworking.com*, or visit some coworking websites, such as LooseCubes (*www.loosecubes.com*), NextSpace (*www.nextspace.us*), Open Desks (*www.opendesks.com*), or The Hub (*www.the-hub.net*).

Working Overseas

You may have searched for jobs in your preferred field all over your city and your entire state. Heck, you may even have sent your resume all over the country. When that failed to yield you any job offers, you may have rewritten your resume and targeted other, less-desirable fields. Still nothing.

What about *really* broadening your job search? Even if the whole country is facing an economic recession and job shortage, there are still parts of the world where prospects are bright and where your talents and abilities may be welcomed with open arms. Despite appearances where you may live, the economy usually isn't terrible everywhere.

Even though the West has suffered an economic decline, the so-called BRIC countries (Brazil, Russia, India, and China) have been experiencing greater economic growth and renewal. Are you intrepid enough to try your luck in some of these distant locations? Australia and Canada are two other countries where the economies seem to be in better shape than many parts of the world. Many of our ancestors pulled up roots in order to seek better opportunities in the United States when their prospects seemed bleak in their home countries. Why not consider adopting that same can-do spirit and seeking employment in the corners of the world where opportunities now seem brightest for your generation?

You may have a skill set that would be in high demand in some of these developing countries. The knowledge that you gain by working in one of those economic powerhouses can then serve you well and differentiate you from other job applicants upon your return. (Unless, of course, you like it so much overseas that you decide to stay!) Even if you don't think that you possess highly specific job skills yet, you may be able to find a position teaching English in one of these foreign locations. You may be able to serve as an international *au pair* (nanny) or find seasonal work that will contribute to building your CV while enabling you to earn money and develop your foreign language skills. If you're lucky, your position may even provide housing, eliminating one of your major living expenses.

If you are willing to consider this option, begin your search with InterExchange. This resource can help explain the logistics of working abroad and connect you with work opportunities and job placement in many foreign countries, including Australia, New Zealand, Argentina, Turkey, Ecuador, Ghana, India, Peru, and more. Their website is *www.interexchange.org/workingabroad*.

There is even the possibility that you may be able to work for an overseas company without leaving the country—if you can land a telecommuting job with a foreign employer. Right now, the most promising fields for telecommuting work include information technology, translation, sales, customer service, and health care data. To learn more about this possibility, try starting with *www.flexjobs.com*.

AmeriCorps

Some government-run organizations can enable college graduates to put their idealism into practice while obtaining work experience and earning living expenses. If you join AmeriCorps, you will find opportunities to address critical needs in communities all across the country. Depending on your placement, you could help fight illiteracy, provide job placement assistance to unemployed people, or assist with urgent disaster response. Full-time AmeriCorps members who complete their service receive an education award that can be used to pay back college loans; members who serve part-time receive a partial award.

The government's official website advertises that if you join AmeriCorps, you will "be able to pay your bills," you will receive "help with college costs and student loans," and you will gain "professional development and job experience." AmeriCorps is also recognized as a public service job for the purposes of the Public Service Loan Forgiveness program.

AmeriCorps consists of three main programs: AmeriCorps State and National, AmeriCorps VISTA, and AmeriCorps NCCC. AmeriCorps State and National is the largest AmeriCorps program, and provides funds to local and national organizations to address critical community needs. Members may serve full- or part-time for less than a year, and those who complete their service will receive funds that can be used to repay student loans. AmeriCorps VISTA (Volunteers in Service to America) offers college graduates the opportunity to help fight poverty through a number of programs. You must commit to a year of full-time service and in return will receive benefits such as a modest living allowance, health care, student loan forbearance or deferment while in service, and a year of eligibility to compete for certain government jobs for which only federal employees are eligible. You will also qualify for a post-service stipend that can be used to help repay student loans or for future education.

AmeriCorps NCCC (National Civilian Community Corps) is a team-based residential program for men and women ages eighteen to twenty-four. This program involves working with nonprofit organizations to complete service projects throughout the region as assigned. You must be willing to relocate and travel where you are needed. In return, you are eligible to receive a living allowance, housing, meals, "limited medical benefits," uniforms, and an educational award upon successful completion of the program. To learn more about the specifics of these programs and application and eligibility requirements and benefits, visit *www.americorps.gov*.

The Peace Corps

The Peace Corps began in the 1960s through the initiation of President (then Senator) John F. Kennedy. He challenged college students to serve their country in the cause of peace by living and working in developing countries. The Peace Corps is now an agency of the federal government devoted to world peace and friendship. Volunteers serve in seventy-six countries in Africa, Asia, the Caribbean, Central and South America, Europe, the Pacific Islands, and the Middle East for twenty-seven months. The Peace Corps offers six main program areas:

1. **Education**

2. **Youth and community development**

3. **Health**

4. **Business and information and communications technology**

5. **Agriculture**

6. **Environment**

The benefits of being a Peace Corps volunteer include a living allowance, medical and dental care, affordable health insurance for up to eighteen months following service, transition funds ($7,425 in 2012), and student loan deferment or possible cancellation. You can learn more about volunteering with the Peace Corps at *www.peacecorps.gov.*

Teach for America

Teach for America employs recent college graduates who commit to teach for two years in "under-resourced urban and rural public schools." You work as a full-time teacher in a low-income community and receive a full salary and comprehensive health benefits from your school district. In addition, most Teach for America Corps members are eligible to receive an education award of up to $11,100 after successfully completing their assignment. You can use these funds to repay qualified student loans or for further education. You could also qualify for loan forbearance and paid interest of qualified student loans. To learn more about Teach for America opportunities and the application procedure, visit *www.teachforamerica.org.*

The Military

When most people hear about college students joining the military they think of undergraduate ROTC programs, but in times of a stagnating economy more college graduates flock to recruitment offices to enlist. Joining the military is obviously a very big decision. Military personnel make a big commitment and face real risks, but they also have the opportunity to serve their country in a number of admirable capacities. In return for their service, they receive substantial benefits, including advanced job training, tax-free housing and food allowances or free room and board, thirty vacation days per year, health and dental care, and various educational benefits.

Having a college degree entitles you to specific additional benefits that may make it attractive for you to consider joining the military. As a college graduate, you are eligible to apply for Officer Candidate School, unlike a high school graduate. You may also qualify for college loan repayment of up to $65,000, along with GI Benefits to help pay for further graduate-level education. If you choose not to use your GI Benefits, you may be able to pass those benefits on to your spouse or children. If you would like to continue your education while serving in the armed forces, you would qualify for tuition assistance, which would pay 100 percent of your tuition while you are on active duty.

If you are interested in learning more about the specific job opportunities and benefits that may be available to you in the armed forces, you should speak to a recruiter directly. Google "military recruiter" in your town and state to find the contact information for all branches of the service in your local area. Listen to what the recruiter has to say and be sure to ask lots of questions. Take and review all of their published information and speak to some active and retired military personnel for their advice before reaching a decision. Most would be more than happy to tell you about their experiences so that you can make an informed choice. This is not a decision to be made in haste, but it is certainly an option to research and consider as you decide on your future path.

SUB-COLLEGE-LEVEL EMERGENCY WORK

Right off the bat, let's take a quick look at where the most job openings are right now. According to the Bureau of Labor Statistics' Office of Occupational Statistics and Employment Projections, here are the top twenty fields, in terms of overall hiring:

Table 2.1	
Occupation	Number of openings, nationally
Cashiers	171,990
Retail salespeople	162,690
Waiters and waitresses	146,620
Customer service representatives	110,840
Registered nurses	103,900

Table 2.1

Occupation	Number of openings, nationally
Food preparation, including fast food	96,720
Office clerks	77,090
Freight laborers	74,580
Elementary school teachers	59,650
Stock clerks and order fillers	56,260
Truck drivers	55,460
Janitors	55,300
Postsecondary teachers	55,290
Home health aides	55,270
Childcare workers	52,310
General operations managers	50,220
Accountants and auditors	49,750
Office supervisors	48,900
Receptionists and information clerks	48,020
Personal and home-care aides	47,780

Obviously, not all of these jobs require a college degree, but they are plentiful and some college graduates will have to take work in these fields until other jobs open up for them. So, let's discuss some of these options for finding immediate employment.

Coffee Shops, Bartending, Waiting Tables, and Hospitality

Okay, I know what you're thinking: I didn't go to college so that I could be a waitress or a bartender! Well, it happens more often than you probably realize, which is why the sympathetic character of "the overqualified restaurant server" has been a TV comedy staple since Diane Chambers tied on her *Cheers* apron in 1982. Many people forget that the original premise of the sitcom *Friends* revolved around the fact that Jennifer Aniston was stuck serving coffee and muffins at the Central Perk Café because she couldn't find a better job. Her "friends" merely gathered there to offer her support. More recently, *2 Broke Girls* has brought the same basic storyline back to prime time. My point is, it happens, and it's not the end of the world. You might even enjoy it. You are not the first person to land in this situation, and you will not be the last. Bartenders can actually make surprisingly good money, and learning to mix drinks and serve customers is a useful skill set that can be valuable for entertaining in any setting, including a corporate one. You can polish your people skills and your communication abilities in a food service or hospitality setting. There are international bar environments where foreign language skills would be valuable. Plus, a good, honest day's work never hurt anyone. Also, you never know who you might meet in a bar or restaurant who could someday open doors for you—especially if you do a very good job.

Jobs in the restaurant industry are generally in plentiful supply and accessible. Food and hospitality are huge industries with constant turnover, so they are nearly always hiring. These jobs often offer flexible scheduling that can be adjusted to accommodate job interviews or additional schooling you may wish to pursue. You may be able to work days, nights, or weekends only, or a combination, according to your preference.

By the way, if you pay attention, you will notice that each bar, restaurant, or coffee shop is a business enterprise competing for survival in the economic marketplace and encompassing a range of functions. You can gain exposure to a number of valuable job skills in a service job, including management, marketing, customer service, and accounting. I will discuss ways to maximize these often-overlooked opportunities in Chapter 4, "The Success Mindset in Any Economy."

Retail Work

Just as with jobs in food service and hospitality, retail jobs are usually in plentiful supply and fairly easy to obtain. Although they typically do not pay well, retail positions in large chain stores may offer college graduates upward mobility into managerial positions. When evaluating a job possibility, be sure to consider the potential for advancement as carefully as the entry-level position itself. As an employee, you may also qualify for discounts on purchases, which is often an appealing side benefit to working in one of your favorite stores.

Call Centers

Nearly all national and international companies use call centers to deal directly with their customers. These positions tend to experience a lot of turnover, so there is an ongoing need for a steady supply of new employees. Previous experience is generally not required. No, it's not glamorous work, but these jobs can be relatively easy to acquire and can teach you valuable customer service, problem-solving, and computer skills. You will learn how to present yourself professionally and how to deal with difficult people in a call center job, and these skills will serve you well in any future position. If you work in sales, you will learn how to handle and overcome rejection. In customer service, you will learn to deal with complaints and resolve sticky situations. Call centers can often offer steady work, at rates between $11 and $18 an hour, and may include health insurance. Scheduling is usually flexible, and sometimes you can even work from home.

Most companies will be looking for people with good telephone and communication skills along with computer experience and typing ability. This eliminates competition from many older workers who may be resistant to dealing with technology. As with all entry-level jobs, approach work in a call center professionally and look for opportunities to advance within the organization.

Live-in Help

You need a job and a place to live. What if you could kill two birds with one stone? You can if you become a "live-in" helper. Many two-income families appreciate having a young, reliable, college-educated person watching their young children at home rather than having to place them in a daycare. On the other end of the age spectrum, there is a high demand for capable people to assist elderly people with their daily living needs, such as cooking and running errands. An arrangement such as this solves the work and living accommodation problem simultaneously. You can find this sort of work by registering with an agency (*www.visitingangels.com* or *www.nannypoppinz.com* are two national ones, but you will be able to find local ones by searching in your area), by advertising your services on Craigslist or community bulletin boards, or through word of mouth through your network of relatives and acquaintances.

This is probably a good time to point out that if you have federal student loans to repay, the government now offers loan forgiveness if you are willing to work in certain "public service" fields for a specified period of time. This can include working in licensed daycare facilities or assisting the elderly. This program may encourage you to broaden the range of jobs you will consider, which is exactly what the government intends. I provide more detailed information on public service loan forgiveness in Chapter 5, which covers your student loan repayment options.

BROADEN YOUR DEFINITION OF A "GOOD JOB"

For a long time, the average American's definition of a "good job" went something like this: A "good job" is one where you don't have to do any physical labor. It involves working with your brain instead of with your body. It occurs in an office under fluorescent lighting (and possibly in a cubicle) and provides employer-sponsored benefits. It is "secure."

Today, many of those "secure" jobs have disappeared, and the most reliable jobs may, instead, be the ones that require you to work with your hands. A "good job" right now may be one that can't be offshored because it has to be performed locally. The reason for this has to do with globalization, which is sending many jobs to the location with the cheapest labor.

Work that must be completed on site, with your hands, can't possibly be outsourced to a foreign country. Workers in other countries obviously can't clean your teeth, cut your hair, deliver your groceries, repair your toilet, or fix your car's brakes. That work has to be done here. Therefore, some of the most secure jobs right now are precisely the types of jobs that previous generations sometimes sneered at—things like auto mechanic, heating and air conditioning repair, and even truck driver.

These are not normally the types of jobs associated with college educations, but they can be satisfying, high paying, and secure and may even allow you to run your own business, which can be both lucrative and satisfying. If you remove your preconceptions about the type of work that college graduates "should" do, you may suddenly see all sorts of possibilities available to you, assuming you are willing to pursue some additional, specialized training. In fact, the news media has reported on the phenomenon of more college-educated workers "jumping tracks" to become manual laborers.

It can be a smart move for some people and you should not reflexively dismiss this possibility. Give it some thought, do your research, and be open-minded and fair in your evaluation before reaching your conclusions. Most importantly, don't be swayed by old-fashioned notions of what a "good job" should be. A good job is work that you enjoy and that provides you with the ability to pay your bills and enjoy a comfortable, reliable lifestyle. Period.

CHAPTER THREE

EVERYDAY SURVIVAL

As an unemployed college grad, every penny counts, and you are going to need to learn to pinch them all. You need to stretch your money as far as it will go, so you are going to have to figure out ways to keep your daily expenses low. First off, here is my suggested list of things you simply don't need:

- **Bottled water**

- **Fancy coffee**

- **Restaurant dinners**

- **Alcohol**

I'm sorry, but until you can cover your mandatory expenses like rent, utilities, health insurance, loan repayments, and transportation, those items are unaffordable luxuries. You might also have to consider watching your favorite televisions shows on Hulu rather than cable or satellite, because those recurring monthly charges will destroy your budget. On the other hand, it would be very difficult for you to operate your job search without a cell phone or an Internet connection, so those items may need to be considered fixed expenses.

If you can't afford to rent your own place you will have two options: move in with family or share living accommodations with roommates. There are unexpected benefits (along with difficulties) to each of these alternatives. By sharing an apartment with roommates, you can cut your living expenses in half or more, while hopefully gaining a friend and companion. By living with family, you will need to renegotiate roles and expectations and contribute to running the household in a more mature way than you probably did when you were in high school. Hopefully, you will also gain the love and support of devoted relatives committed to helping you get launched professionally.

When you are in the difficult position of not earning enough money to pay your keep, you must ruthlessly slash every cost that you can. This means that virtually everything is up for consideration, including clothes, entertainment, and travel. You must question and eliminate every possible expense—especially recurrent monthly ones. Are there any features of your cell phone plan you can ditch? Be mindful of your minutes and terms so that you don't get hit with unexpected extra charges. Can you negotiate a cheaper Internet connection, reduce your car insurance payment or, better yet, rely on public transportation or a bike for getting around?

I hope you will not view this as a painful exercise. I actually find slashing bills to be quite fun and liberating. A couple of times a year, I make a habit of calling my utility providers and threatening to switch to another service unless they lower my rate. They nearly always do, and then I feel triumphant—a small victory for the consumer over giant corporations. The lower your monthly living expenses, the more freedom you will have in the rest of your budget. This is a very useful life skill that will serve you well as you assume future responsibilities such as marriage, home ownership, business management, or parenthood. If you can figure out how to eliminate wasteful expenditures now, and really slash your expenses to the bone, you will become a very savvy consumer who will be able to afford to accomplish more of your cherished goals in life.

Here are some more suggestions:

- **Use the public library for books and videos.**

- **Buy generic, store brands rather than name brands at the supermarket.**

- **Stock up on necessary items, such as toiletries, when they're on sale.**

- **Shop for clothes and other durable items at garage sales and Goodwill; it's where all the "hipsters" buy now, anyway.**

- **Go "shopping" in your own closet and make new combinations out of your existing clothes.**

- **Arrange a clothing swap with your other unemployed friends, so that you can all exchange items and freshen up your own wardrobes.**

- **Be mindful of your energy usage to lower your utility costs. Candles are very chic, just as long as you don't burn anything down.**

Once you start searching for money saving ideas, they will begin to snowball, and it can become an exciting challenge.

Cheap is good, but free is even better. Believe it or not, there are people online advertising to give things away! You may be able to find free furniture, clothes, televisions, bicycles—who knows what—at *www.freecycle.org*. This website is dedicated to reducing the amount of waste in landfills by encouraging people to share unwanted items rather than discarding them. Be sure to check there first before making a new purchase.

LOOK AT FOOD IN A NEW WAY

Stay home and cook, rather than eating out. This is not just a great way to save money, but it is also a vital life skill that you need to develop, anyway. When it's time to splurge on a restaurant meal, be selective not just about where you will eat, but also when. When my husband and I were both in graduate school, we figured out that eating out for lunch was generally much less expensive than eating out for dinner. Lunch often costs about 40 percent less than dinner prices at the same restaurants. We could afford to eat lunches in a lot of expensive restaurants where we couldn't afford to buy dinners. Even today when our finances are much more secure, we still prefer to avoid the dinner crowds and pick up a cheaper lunch special instead. We also find the lunch-sized portions much more appropriate, and it's a healthier time of day to be eating than late in the evening. Dinner portions are generally oversized, anyway. Normally, when we do go out for dinner, we end up with two Styrofoam containers of leftovers in the refrigerator, which aren't nearly as appealing the next day.

Drink tap water. Having worked as a waitress in high school and college, I learned that the biggest mark-up item in a restaurant is beverages. We have made it a lifelong habit to only order water in restaurants, and we have taught our children to do the same. At a conservative estimate of $2 per drink, I believe my family has easily saved five figures in restaurant beverages over the past twenty years, while improving our health in the bargain. No one needs the junk calories of sugary soft drinks, not to mention the added expense. As for having a bottle of water around with you all day, try a refillable canteen. It keeps water colder longer, and reduces plastic waste.

If you'd rather share dinner with friends than lunch, invite them over for a home-cooked meal instead of going to a restaurant. Attend free events, which are frequently listed in your local newspapers, and take up affordable hobbies like hiking, biking, and visiting museums. Make gifts rather than buying them. This is classier and much more meaningful, anyway.

Learn to garden. This can be an extremely satisfying hobby and even a crucial survival skill. Homegrown vegetables are free from pesticides and other harmful additives, and there's something deeply satisfying about vegetables grown by your own labor. It also provides exercise and fresh air, to say nothing of improving your knowledge of plants.

Buy generic store brands, which are often better quality than name brands. For fun, rather than going to the movies—an expensive form of entertainment—play board games with a group of friends.

FRUGAL IS CHIC

Thrift is becoming trendy again, after a decade of embarrassing excess fueled by unaffordable credit. Saving money is not only fashionable, but it's also better for the environment. It can even be good for the soul, as financial limits have a way of helping us discover simple pleasures and appreciate all the good things we already have in our lives rather than trying to chase happiness through the pursuit of material items.

Cutting expenses can even be good for your career, when you build your social events calendar around free or affordable networking opportunities such as events held by your local Chamber of Commerce (whose membership dues may be tax-deductible) or career-targeted groups sponsored by *www.meetup.com*, a free online group helping people connect over common interests. This is a great two-for-one deal. You get the fun of socializing at organized events, which often include free food, while adding to your list of potential career contacts. This can be a very cost-effective way to combine business and pleasure, as many career experts point out that 50 percent of job opportunities are never advertised; they are filled by acquaintances who hear about the open positions first. This is why constant networking is crucial. Luckily, it can also be an affordable way of filling your social calendar.

Once you start pinching pennies, it can become quite addictive. You may start to find increasingly creative ways to squeeze more value from every dollar and you may begin to find yourself shocked at the ways in which others squander their money and the world's resources, as well. What a waste! If you develop the thrifty habit now, you will probably have a hard time giving it up, even when you start earning more money. Then you will be able to save the remainder. Thrift is an important part of living a more sustainable, ecologically respectful lifestyle, so your efforts won't just help your personal budget: they can also have a positive impact on the environment for future generations. In other words, you can save green by going green. For more ideas on ways to trim costs, avoid waste, and save additional money, try *www.101waystosavemoney.com* or *www.beingfrugal.net*.

WHY THE CRASH OF THE REAL ESTATE MARKET IS GOOD NEWS FOR YOU

One actual bright spot in the economy I would like to point out to you is the precipitous crash of real estate prices. This is bad news for older property owners, but great news for young people who need an affordable place to live. Let's take a moment to feel sorry for all the "underwater" homeowners out there, as well as for the countless purchasers of overpriced homes who have now lost them to foreclosure. Okay, time's up: now pounce on these opportunities!

While previous generations struggled for decades with rising home prices that spiraled out of control and destroyed their budgets, today's young adults now enjoy the opportunity to purchase real estate at bargain-basement prices. This is one very bright light for you in a rather bleak economy. Low-cost real estate offers the potential to make your fixed living expenses very manageable, if you play your cards right. If you are in the enviable position of being able to purchase a property, you may be able to pick up a foreclosure at a ridiculously low price. It is definitely a buyer's market out there and you should play hardball when you negotiate. If you can't afford to buy, the huge numbers of vacancies should also make rents more affordable in many locations. Here again, you should expect and demand affordable rents and if you don't receive them, then you should take your business elsewhere, because in most areas of the country, it is also a renter's market. If the landlords in your area will not budge on their prices, then move to a different area where renters hold the upper hand.

Buy with Friends

If you know several other unemployed young people in need of affordable housing, you could even spot a potential business opportunity. You might be able to finance the purchase of a property and then collect rents and make a profit by acting as the landlord for your roommates. You could purchase a duplex, live in one half, and rent the other half. Obviously, you would need to do your homework and ensure that the money you collect from renters would cover all of the costs of carrying the property, including the mortgage, taxes, insurance, and maintenance. (Here is a great rule of thumb to keep you from getting in over your head with real estate: if you purchase a rental property for $100,000, you need to be able to collect $1,000 a month in rents to cover your expenses. If the purchase price is $95,000, then you'd better be able to rent it for $950 a month, and so on. So check what the going rental rates are in your area before deciding whether a potential property is a good deal or not.) If you can derive a positive cash flow from a property rental situation like this, then you could conceivably enjoy a reliable passive income for years!

SHOULD I GO BACK TO SCHOOL FOR MORE EDUCATION?

At some point, most unemployed, or underemployed, college graduates will wonder whether they should return to school for more education. You may have concluded that your current hiring prospects are grim without a graduate degree. You may have decided that you want to pursue a specific occupation with specialized educational requirements. Or, you may have enjoyed college and find your memories of it preferable to the harsh alternative of being in the "real" world facing difficult employment odds.

BY THE NUMBERS

Many unemployed graduates return to graduate school with the hope of becoming college professors. According to MindingtheCampus.com, right now is a terrible time for new PhDs. Writer Charlotte Allen says today's doctoral graduates, especially in the humanities, face "a job market where fewer than one out of every two holders of doctoral degrees in the humanities these days receive job offers that put them onto the tenure track that is key to a successful (if seldom wealth-generating) and reasonably secure life of teaching and scholarship—and that's in a good year. Right now we're in a bad year, when, according to the

American Association of University Professors, the ratio of tenure-track openings to new doctorates is more like 1 to 4." Likewise, a dean at New York University told the *New York Times* in 2009 that unemployed PhDs looking for jobs are stacked up "like planes hovering over La Guardia."

The answer is not simple, and all I can say is that it depends. First of all, you should face the fact that going back to school is not always the right answer. It has to make economic sense. Sometimes, people go back to graduate school simply because they have been in school their whole lives, so the classroom seems like a comfortable, familiar setting. In times of stress, they want to return somewhere where they feel "safe" and where they understand the expectations. Higher education offers a clear set of guidelines for making progress and a clear reward upon completion: another degree. This sense of certitude is very appealing when you feel like you are having trouble moving forward. The value of the additional degree in the marketplace, however, needs to be a major consideration in your deliberations.

Graduate School

If you are looking at graduate school as a place where you can hide from or postpone your financial problems for a few years, then there is a very real chance that it could actually make the problem worse. Should you choose your field unwisely and finance the degree with student loans, then you could find yourself in a few years still unemployed, but with even larger debts to repay. This is simply a more expensive version of your current dilemma. So, graduate school is not a place to try to escape from economic realities. A higher degree may even make you "overqualified" for some available positions and you'll be even less employable than before you enrolled.

I am *not* saying that you should not go back to school, but I am saying that you need to have a very well-thought-out plan with a clearly defined payoff and high likelihood of success (defined here as employment) afterward before signing up for more years of higher education. You need an exit strategy; wishful thinking isn't good enough, as you should have learned from your entry into the real world from college.

There are worthwhile graduate school opportunities, but please do considerable career research before signing up for something as expensive and time-consuming (some PhD programs can last a *decade*) as a doctoral program. Despite the fact that official lists of future job opportunities list "postsecondary teacher" near the top, so far these hoped-for faculty positions do not seem to be materializing. The reasons for this include higher education budget cuts, delayed retirements, a shift to low-paid adjunct instructors, and the rise of online education. You must do your research before committing to something as arduous and grueling as a master's or doctoral program or other professional degree. Be very thorough and consider not just your interests but also future job demand.

To find out what the actual job prospects are like in academia, you will want to review the listings in the *Chronicle of Higher Education* (see *www.chronicle.com/jobs*). I would also suggest that you read the editorials and opinion pieces in the *Chronicle*, many of which deal with recruitment and hiring, to get a sense of the current job climate. Most importantly, talk to people working in the field directly, so that you get up-to-date information from people closest to the action.

Law School

Law school is another area in which many graduates are currently facing expensive disappointment. A recent analysis by the *Wall Street Journal* found that law school grads have roughly a fifty–fifty chance of landing a job as a lawyer. Those aren't great odds. Currently, there are more than a dozen lawsuits against various law schools filed by disgruntled, unemployed graduates. The first case was thrown out by New York Supreme Court Justice Melvin Schweitzer, who acknowledged that we are seeing the "most severe contraction in demand for legal services this court can recall since the early 1970s." Nevertheless, the judge then put the burden for making smart educational choices squarely on the backs of the graduates and insinuated that they should have known better than to overpay for their law degrees in a down economy. In his decision, he asserted that college graduates "are a sophisticated subset of education consumers, capable of sifting through data and weighing alternatives before making a decision regarding their post-college options." In other words, *caveat emptor*: let the buyer beware.

Before pursuing any postgraduate training, you must do your homework and exercise due diligence. Be sure to ask what the placement rates are for graduates of the programs you are considering and what sort of practical help the instructors, institution, and alumni will provide you in seeking suitable employment afterward. Conduct a thorough investigation before agreeing to invest your limited time and money in an educational program, no matter how prestigious it may seem. Don't rely on hearsay or past performance to reach your decisions; consider future employability first and foremost and research the facts.

CHECK OUT ALL YOUR OPTIONS

Should you decide to pursue further education, always look for the most affordable way to earn the credential. To give you one example, I was able to earn my master's degree at no cost because I found a job working as a "research assistant" (glorified term for typist) at the university where my husband was studying at the time. One day, my boss informed me that as an employee of the university, I was entitled to take free courses; I took advantage of that opportunity and signed right up. I worked part-time while attending school part-time. Ultimately, I was offered a graduate assistantship in my academic program, which allowed me to then work as a career counselor while completing my counseling degree for free. In this way I gained valuable job experience. So, check first for clerical or other jobs at the universities you hope to attend if you harbor hopes of adding some initials after your name.

In most fields (excluding professional programs like medicine, law, and most MBA programs), you shouldn't have to pay for your graduate degree; instead, you should be able to negotiate for a teaching or research assistantship that typically includes tuition waivers and a small living stipend. Most graduate departments have a limited number of these so-called "funded" positions, but they will accept some additional students who are willing to pay cash for the credits.

I would encourage you to consider only graduate opportunities with tuition waivers, unless money is truly no object for you (in which case, you are reading the wrong book). Graduate assistantships are a way in which certain disciplines try to restrict the number of new scholars who will be admitted to the field, to avoid producing too many discontented graduates unable to find suitable work. So, if you are not being offered a graduate assistantship, consider it your warning that down the line you might not be offered employment in this field.

Incidentally, most college graduates think that the only way to go back to school is by attending the next highest level of education—graduate school. I would like to encourage you to consider another option that may prove far less expensive, less time-consuming, and possibly more effective in terms of jumpstarting your career: community or technical colleges. You could consider this a lateral move, rather than a forward pass, but just as in football, it can sometimes prove surprisingly and unexpectedly effective in moving you forward.

You may be thinking: What? But community colleges and technical colleges are for students who couldn't get into a "real" college! Well, guess what? A lot of their graduates are finding decent-paying jobs right now, because they have very specific job training in high-demand fields. They have earned licensures required to qualify for certain restricted openings. A search of anticipated job openings requiring some postsecondary training below the bachelor's degree level reveals some very interesting results:

Table 3.1	
Occupation	Number of openings, nationally
Registered nurse	103,900
Licensed practical nurse	39,130
Computer support specialist	23,460
Hairdresser, cosmetologist	21,950
Auto service technician/ mechanic	18,170
Preschool teacher	17,830
Insurance sales agent	15,260

Table 3.1	
Occupation	Number of openings, nationally
Heating, air conditioning mechanic	13,620
Real estate agent	12,830
Welder	12,630
Fitness trainer	12,380
Paralegal	10,400
Dental hygienist	9,840

Source: www.careeronestop.org

These jobs require two years of training or less and come with fairly bright career prospects. Some of them pay quite well. Don't discount the possibility of becoming a so-called "reverse transfer" who attends community college or technical school after already graduating from college. This is not as rare as you might think. These days, college graduates are actually becoming the majority in some technical training programs. According to *Inside Higher Ed*, the recession has created a surge in community college enrollments because it can be an affordable way of adding "career-friendly" credentials and specialized skills to your resume. Before signing up for a lengthy, expensive graduate school program, you should certainly investigate all career-training avenues that might be shorter and less costly.

Working with Your Hands

Technical training programs, by definition, are meant to show you how to work with your hands or with tools or other specialized implements. Matthew Crawford, in his book *Shop Class as Soulcraft: An Inquiry into the Value of Work*, describes not only the practicality of learning to work with your hands, but also the "psychic satisfactions" of it. Crawford, who holds a doctorate in political science, worked for several years in a Washington think tank, only to find himself dispirited and bored, unable to see what tangible value he was producing. He quit and discovered his passion when he rekindled his lifelong interest in motorcycles and wound up opening his own shop, where he now produces "real products." He even finds mechanical work intellectually stimulating, as he is forced to solve difficult problems using practical wisdom.

=BY THE NUMBERS=

Even in the midst of a major recession with high unemployment rates, some employers still can't find people with the right skills . . . or with the ability or drive to even learn them! A report released by Deloitte consultants and the National Association of Manufacturers details how American manufacturers have 600,000 unfilled positions because of a lack of qualified, skilled workers. As explained in the *Financial Times,* one company in Baltimore can't grow due to their inability to find qualified employees. Despite advertising a salary of more than $80,000 with overtime, with health and pension benefits, Marlin Steel Wire Products can't find qualified applicants able or willing to complete the required training.

Oddly enough, according to this article, employment vacancies (defined as the number of advertised, unfilled positions) have risen by 35 percent since 2009, even while the national unemployment rate has remained high. This could signal a significant mismatch between the jobs employers have to offer and the skills possessed by workers. To find a job in this economy, you're going to have to pursue the type of training that is currently in demand— it's as simple as that.

$

Credentialing

You should also look into credentialing opportunities, which are generally shorter and more focused than graduate degrees. Many specific credentials are valued highly by potential employers and they may provide a more direct route to a job than academia. Some of these are offered through trade associations and professional organizations, others by community or technical colleges, and some by traditional colleges and universities. For instance, Harvard University's Extension School offers certificates in nanotechnology, religious studies, strategic management, sustainability, and web technologies. This focused career training can lead to a professional certificate in just five courses. According to the extension school, many potential students ask: "What's the value of a certificate?" Their answer: "Certificates are one of the fastest growing credentials in postsecondary education. The value of the certificate is in its specialized topic and concentrated coursework. Demonstrate to employers that you now have knowledge in a relevant field. By gaining this expertise, you can add greater value to the organization's mission and bottom line." To learn more about available credentialing possibilities, visit the Credentialing Center at *www.careeronestop.org/credentialing/credentialing home.asp.* My view is that some of the best credentials come from trade organizations, because these programs provide you with a way to meet and network with individuals working in the field, so you should also research and reach out to these established groups.

Always conduct thorough research before investing in any educational or certification program. You've already been through one degree program without landing a job— don't make it two! The main aspect to evaluate is your likelihood of finding desirable employment upon completion. Be on the lookout for on-the-job-training opportunities, as these are the most affordable way of building your skills. As a college graduate, you obviously have demonstrated that you have the ability to learn. Now, put it to use learning a skill that employers will pay for.

Over the years, I have heard many community college and technical program educators complain that they have plenty of good jobs available to graduates, but they have a hard time attracting qualified students, due to the "snob" factor. We seem to have accepted the notion that working with our hands is somehow less valuable or less respectable than working with our minds—although plumbers, chefs, nurses, and mechanics work with both, and their services are generally in high demand and well paid. Many can also become independent, successful, and creative business owners while many college graduates spend their entire careers working as others' employees. Plus, working with one's hands is certainly preferable to not working at all!

I recently watched a very funny episode of the TV show *Community* in which John Goodman guest-starred as the Vice Dean in charge of Heating and Air Conditioning Repair. When the Dean of the college paid him a visit, he was stunned to learn that the air conditioning program "has a job placement rate five times higher than the rest of the school combined," is responsible for most of the school's funding, and that "graduates of this school are guaranteed lucrative employment for their entire lives." Art imitates life. During a recent ten-hour-long drive along I-95, I spent several hours following an AC repair truck whose painted sign advertised "Immediate Hiring Bonuses! Call Today!"

I'm not suggesting you rush off to go into air conditioning repair, but I am suggesting that you shouldn't disregard the possibility outright. Open your mind to alternative ways to make a good living.

You should closely examine the opportunities that your local technical or community college has to offer and evaluate them objectively before deciding on your path. For instance, despite all the talk of a decline in American manufacturing, machinists are currently in high demand with very bright prospects and solid pay—starting around $30 an hour. That's enough to raise a family on. By adding specific training or licensure to your current diploma, you may greatly improve your hiring prospects in a short period of time, and at a reasonable cost, while remaining an excellent candidate for future promotions into the managerial ranks, thanks to your college degree.

My point is: Somebody is hiring. You need to figure out who it is and prepare yourself to compete for those positions. A clue: think of things that everybody needs and that are not optional. You may not have thought that you were interested in learning a manual trade, or working in health care, but we all have to do what needs to be done to survive in a difficult economy. Even if studying for certification or an associate's degree in dental hygiene or MRI technology is below the level of a bachelor's degree, if it leads to a high-paying job that you enjoy, what do you care? Rest assured that your undergraduate education will not have gone to waste. You will use that knowledge base to excel in your coursework and in any employment position you take.

Community colleges are always going to be looking for the next generation of instructors, as well, so your specialized training could even lead you into a postsecondary teaching career in a specialized field without having to earn a doctorate degree. You might find some wonderful surprises by traveling down the less-traveled road.

CAN YOU QUALIFY FOR WELFARE OR FOOD STAMPS?

It is possible that during your temporary, involuntary sojourn as an unemployed college graduate you will need financial help beyond what you can acquire by working a survival job. Despite your best efforts, you may not be able to find even sub-college-level emergency work, and you may be unable to pay for even the most basic life necessities. Your family may be unable or unwilling to help you financially, and you may require assistance.

As a recent graduate, you probably will not qualify for unemployment benefits. It is also unlikely that you will be eligible for welfare benefits, as these are generally not intended for single persons with no dependents, unless you have some sort of disability.

You may, however, qualify for food stamps. The Supplemental Nutrition Assistance Program is designed to help low-income people buy food. If you are not earning enough money to buy adequate food, then that means you. You can learn more about food stamps at *www.ssa.gov/pubs/10101.html* or by calling 1-800-772-1213.

Although food stamps is a federal program, it is administered by state or local agencies.

You must meet certain requirements to qualify. Essentially, you must have limited resources and meet an income limit. You can apply for food stamps at any Social Security Administration office. You will need to provide identification, and you may be asked to provide rent receipts or records of your utility costs. The government provides a prescreening eligibility tool to give you an indication of whether or not you may qualify for food stamps. You can locate it online at *www.snap-step1.usda.gov/fns.*

You may be expected to register for work or to participate in an employment or training program as a condition of receiving assistance. Regardless of whether or not you qualify for food stamps, as an unemployed graduate you should certainly look into all of the career training opportunities available to you through state or local agencies in your area.

Most states operate either "Career Link" or "Job Link" centers, which are designed to help employees and employers find each other. They can also direct you to available training opportunities and they may host job fairs featuring local employers. To locate the state employment assistance agency in your state, simply Google the name of your state and "Career Link" or "Job Link." Track down and take full advantage of every opportunity your state provides you in finding employment. If you qualify for food stamps, you may also qualify for subsidized training and apprenticeship opportunities, so be sure to ask about all the educational opportunities available to you through these funded agencies.

SEEKING THE HOLY GRAIL: A FULL-TIME JOB WITH BENEFITS

Finally, don't give up on the goal of finding a full-time job with benefits merely because you may have to accept some "emergency" work to tide you over temporarily during your search. Despite all the dismal statistics and pessimistic news stories, some graduates are still getting hired and you should certainly assume that with persistence and a solid work ethic you could be one of them. You must do everything possible to position yourself as an attractive candidate while beating the bushes to hear of any anticipated job opportunities within your preferred fields and firms.

Continue to network actively while building a strong, impressive online presence that will bolster and support your printed resume. Alert all of your family, friends, and extended contacts that you are searching for a suitable position and ask them to let you know if they hear of any upcoming openings. A job isn't going to come find you in this economy. You are going to have to go find it. Stay active, stay visible, maintain your professional appearance and your job skills, and keep applying.

PART II

MANAGING THE FACTS OF LIFE

Benjamin Franklin once quipped that nothing in life is sure except death and taxes. Today, he might have added "student loan payments" and "health insurance premiums" to the list of unavoidable obligations.

It's not easy to take on these responsibilities straight out of college. Flexibility is going to be crucial to your success in the new economy. You need a willingness to face facts, adapt quickly, spot promising trends, read the writing on the wall, squeeze extra value from every dollar, and try unconventional things.

You may need to consider new living and working arrangements and form strategic alliances with others in similar circumstances. Rather than waiting for opportunities to arise, you will probably have to be more assertive in creating opportunities for yourself. And you're going to have to do all of this with an unfailingly positive, winning attitude while simultaneously juggling adulthood's inevitable financial obligations. Daunting? Perhaps. Surmountable? Definitely.

CHAPTER FOUR

THE SUCCESS MINDSET IN ANY ECONOMY

After completing thirteen years of K–12 education, and four (or more) years of higher education—along with all the required homework, assignments, application essays, and tests—you can be forgiven for feeling that you might be entitled to some sort of tangible (preferably monetary) reward at this point. It is understandable if you were hoping to rest on your well-earned academic laurels and coast for a little while. You might feel like the world owes you a little something now. After all, for nearly two decades you have been exhorted to study hard and delay gratification, and you have done just that. The implication of the advice given to you was that all that hard work would lead you to a "good job." And . . . here you are, unemployed or underemployed. It's okay to spend some time licking your wounds and examining your grievances.

Notice that I said "some time." We're not talking years, here. We're talking a couple of weeks or months, tops. That's enough. Then, it's time to get up and get moving. Yes, you can be disappointed. It's okay to feel that way and healthy to admit it, but dwelling on it too long is disempowering. You need to take action. You need to start exactly where you are, with what you have, and do whatever you can to improve your job prospects.

Having difficulty finding your first real job is not going to be the end of the world for your generation. It is merely a starting point—the makings of a great survival story that you will get to tell one day. Try looking at it this way: Instead of having everything handed to you on a silver platter, you have received a gift—you've got to pull yourself up by your bootstraps, and this will make you stronger in the end. To put your struggle into perspective once more, recall that the Depression, World War II, the Korean War, and the Vietnam War generations didn't expect to have their lives interrupted, but that's what happened to them. They dealt with it, recovered, and moved on. You will, too.

It's a mistake to think of completing college as an ending. Your graduation ceremony was called a commencement. The word "commencement" literally means "beginning" because it is the start of something new. Everything up to now was merely a prelude to your entry into the working world, no matter how humbly you have to start. In your case, commencement signals the time for you to roll up your sleeves and get busy, because now the real work actually begins. *Now* is the time for you to really hustle!

I know that you were hoping to cash in your academic chips at the pay-off window of life at this point, but there is simply too much competition for employment right now to allow you to do that. You're going to have to shrug it off and adjust your expectations and your behavior to match reality. So let's talk about some productive strategies and attitudes that will help you move forward into a bright future.

YOU DIDN'T THINK YOU WERE GOING TO START ON TOP, DID YOU?

When you leave college and enter the working world, unfortunately it is like being a freshman all over again. You are the lowest person on the totem pole. As a new entrant to the workforce, you will probably be looking for an entry-level job within an established organization. Entry-level work, by definition, implies that you lack prior experience in the field. Typically, entry-level workers are assigned the least desirable tasks within an organization—sometimes called "grunt" work. This is how you are expected to "learn the ropes" of a business.

This is nothing new. It's the way things have always been in the work world. These organizations are testing your determination and measuring your level of commitment to decide whether you are worthy of receiving more important assignments. Many employers and work supervisors believe that new employees need to prove themselves and "pay their dues" before they receive the best assignments or higher levels of pay.

As a recent graduate this can be a very frustrating attitude to encounter. You may feel as if you already paid your dues in college. You certainly paid your tuition, and you may still be paying it in the form of student loans. You have a lot to offer right now and feel that you aren't being given a chance to fully demonstrate your worth because you are constantly being given such low-level assignments.

You may be right. You probably are capable of much more than running a photocopy machine, answering phones, or making macchiatos. In fact, I'm sure you are. And it's a good bet that your boss knows it, too.

You're still going to have to pay your dues, though. The truth is, you are in competition with a lot of other capable workers for good work. Everybody wants to do the most interesting work, and be paid well for it, but there is only so much desirable work to go around. Those with endurance and patience are most likely to reach the level where they can claim the plum assignments. Remember: no one owes you interesting work. You have to earn it.

You should be aware that, from the perspective of many employers, some college graduates seem to have a sense of great entitlement. It is very annoying for a supervisor to have someone arrive on a new job and suddenly act like he or she is "above" the work that the supervisor used to have to do to reach his current position. New graduates may feel that they have a right to leapfrog over other hardworking employees by virtue of their intelligence and their academic degrees. This is a very frustrating attitude for employers to have to deal with, and it certainly will not endear you to them—or to your coworkers.

Get the Right Attitude for Any Job

Maybe you are disappointed because you had to take a job in food service or retail, just to get by, while you look for a better position. The worst thing you can do is to accept a job and then show up each day with a bad attitude that lets everyone around you know that you think your work is somehow "beneath" you. That kind of behavior won't get you anywhere. A bad mindset will not get you what you want. Instead, it will move you farther away from it.

The Greek philosopher Euripides offered this sage advice: "Slight not what is near though aiming at what is far." By this, he means that it is great to have high aspirations, but that it might take you a while to reach them. In the meantime, pay attention to the tasks that lie right in front of you and appreciate them. Do not show disdain for the work that you have to do on the way to reaching your highest goals. If you do, you will not enjoy the journey and you might not even get where you want to go.

By way of negative example, let's talk about how *not* to succeed in your first job:

- ■ **Show up every day with a surly, condescending attitude. Assume you are better than everyone else at your job and be sure to drop not-so-subtle hints to let them know that you feel you are too good to be working there. Make sure that your body language communicates disgust, or at least abject boredom with the job. Roll your eyes as a silent rebuke to others and sigh loudly, if necessary, to indicate your contempt for them and for your job duties. Complain incessantly about how unfair everything is. Act superior to everyone, including your stupid boss who doesn't know anything.**

- ■ **If your managers and coworkers still don't seem to get the message that you are better than they are, then tell them outright that your job stinks and you deserve better than to be working in this dump. Be sure to act insulted by all of your tasks and assignments. That will surely convince them to start giving you some more important work!**

- ■ **Complete simple tasks sloppily and carelessly, if at all; obviously, they're beneath you and not worthy of your full attention. You are not going to bother showing management what you are capable of**

accomplishing until you start getting some better assignments! Expect your managers to recognize your inward greatness and promote you to the position you deserve when they finally wake up and see how deserving you truly are.

I realize this sounds like that comic "Goofus and Gallant" from the *Highlights* magazines that you probably used to read when you were waiting for your turn at the dentist's office, but please reflect on this the next time you are given a boring work assignment and silently think to yourself: "I went to college for *this*?" Your willingness to complete basic job duties cheerfully and thoroughly communicates volumes about your character and your value to any organization. It may take a while, but you will eventually be noticed and rewarded for your diligence and consistent efforts.

Trust me—no one wants to work with someone who doesn't want to be there. It spoils the atmosphere and makes the entire day unpleasant for everyone. Don't be that person. If you are, your coworkers will dread your arrival and your boss will thwart your advancement. You will only be sabotaging yourself. If you think you're "too good" for your current job, rest assured: you will never have a better one and you may even lose the one you do have.

You are going to be different.

- **You're not going to show up with an attitude of entitlement.**

- **You are going to work hard for everything that you get.**

- **You are going to go above and beyond your assigned duties.**

- **You are going to work cheerfully and be a pleasure to employ.**

Because of all these things, you are going to beat the odds and land a great position, even in a very tough economy. Why? Because there is very little traffic on the extra mile.

You are going to look for opportunities to make your boss look good and show initiative in finding ways to be an outstanding employee. Every employer wants employees who treat the business as though it were their own. You will make it your business to figure out how to make this business function more effectively and then deliver more than you are asked to do.

You are also going to be appreciative and respectful of any organization that offers you the opportunity to work there, even if it merely provides a steppingstone to your next position. This attitude alone will set you far above the rest of the pack, who do the bare minimum just to get by.

You may have to commit to a certain investment of time with your first employer to be taken seriously enough to receive significant responsibilities. For instance, Starbucks expects new employees to work for at least one year before applying for higher positions within the company. This will enable you to build up the "work experience" portion of your resume so that in your next position, you will be able to start at a higher level. Resolve to do so cheerfully.

If you're expecting someone to be impressed with your college degree, forget it. It's not going to happen in this job market. Good jobs are very hard to come by and there are many equally capable graduates competing for every position. You can't take anything for granted. You must go above and beyond in every endeavor and bring something extra to the game. That "something extra" can be your winning, willing attitude.

So, the first thing you may have to do is get over yourself. Yes, a little humility is in order. A steady diet of ramen noodles should help get you off your high horse, should you currently be riding one. Until you prove your worth at the lowest-level tasks, you probably won't have the chance to show what else you can do. Resolve to stay the course with steady determination until you can break through to the next level of employment.

GO WHERE YOU NEED TO GO, DO WHAT IT TAKES

Are you willing to hit the road to find better opportunities? Some regions of the country have better job opportunities than others—a simple matter of supply and demand. To maximize your chances of finding employment, you may have to rethink and compromise some of your expectations, such as where you will live.

BY THE NUMBERS

North and South Dakota have some of the lowest unemployment rates in the country, (3.7 percent and 4.8 percent, respectively, as of late 2012), thanks to an oil boom. Beyond the workers needed to extract the oil, they also need workers in every possible endeavor to support the growing population. Other states with lower-than-average unemployment rates include New Hampshire (5.4 percent), Vermont (5.6 percent), Wyoming (6.2 percent), Hawaii (6.3 percent), Virginia (6.4 percent), and Oklahoma (6.5 percent). Are you willing to move to one of these places to find work?

A CNNMoney article titled "Double your salary in the middle of nowhere, North Dakota," explains that companies in the new oil boomtowns are hiring like crazy, and "you can make $15 an hour serving tacos, $25 an hour waiting tables and $80,000 a year driving trucks." One couple interviewed in the article, who relocated to North Dakota to dig themselves out of debt, says, "It's just so crazy that the rest of the country has no jobs, and here's this one place that doesn't have enough people to fill all the jobs." In Watford City, North Dakota, oil companies are doling out average salaries of $70,000, with overtime pushing many employees over $100,000, while other local business are raising their minimum pay simply to attract the workers they need to operate.

Some entry-level jobs in grocery and convenience stores are offering $12 an hour.

If you think it would be dull to live in North Dakota, it probably won't be for long, with people flocking there from all over the country to earn and spend their high salaries. One radio commentator claimed, "Bismarck is going to be the new Dubai." Housing prices, while rising due to growing demand, are still cheaper than in many metropolitan areas, and many transplants are coming up with creative housing arrangements, such as living in dormlike "mancamps," campers, or RVs. It doesn't sound luxurious, but at least it comes with steady paychecks.

If you're willing to consider a daring move to a far-flung location, it will help to think of it as an exciting adventure rather than an enforced exile to Siberia. As Shakespeare's Hamlet wisely intoned, "There is nothing either good or bad, but thinking makes it so." Generations ago, adventurous young people moved west to the frontier in search of better opportunities, and their exploits became the subject of countless television shows, movies, and novels. Perhaps someday in the future, your generation's exploits and travails will be likewise remembered and romanticized. It certainly makes a more compelling story than hanging around on your parents' couch; just think how amazed your grandchildren will be when you regale them with tales of your exciting youth seeking your fortune in far off places!

Go for the Middle

The Dakotas aren't the only "hot" location for jobs. According to the *Fiscal Times*, which ranks metro areas in the United States by their rate of new job creation, your odds of landing employment are also bright in Fort Wayne, Indiana; Worcester, Massachusetts; Louisville, Kentucky; Tulsa, Oklahoma; Tucson, Arizona; Houston, Texas; Akron, Ohio; and Boise, Idaho. No, these destinations might not be at the top of your "Places to See" list, but with money in your pocket, they're sure to look a lot more appealing. Jerold Leslie writes in Yahoo! Finance that the Midwest is booming and that you can find the places likely to have low unemployment simply by taking a map and drawing a line from Texas straight north to North Dakota. Reporting on data analyzed by Bert Sperling of Sperling's Best Places, this article recommends the Midwest due to the combination of a low cost of living and high commodity prices, which are boosting the region's existing oil, gas, and farming industries. Some more hiring towns to check out include Sioux Falls, South Dakota; Lawton, Oklahoma; Logan, Utah; Lincoln, Nebraska; Fargo, North Dakota; and Iowa City, Iowa. These towns may not sound romantic or exotic, but that doesn't mean they aren't perfectly nice places to live with lots of nice people to meet.

Why not explore the possibility of relocating to the middle of the country? Where's your sense of adventure? Years ago, when the American frontier was being settled, ambitious youth seeking better opportunities in life were advised to "Go West, Young Man!" Today, that advice may need to be rewritten: "Go Midwest, Young Man and Young Woman!" It can pay to leave the predictable path of obvious destinations and check out some unexpected possibilities on your unorthodox job search. To do more research on possible places to relocate, check out Sperling's site at *www.bestplaces.net*.

Remember: you have to go where the jobs are heading now, not where they used to be. Many of these locations suffer from an image problem and have to fight the perception that they are not as appealing as, say, New York or Los Angeles. This can work to your benefit. Employers in these "off-the-beaten-path" locations may be willing to offer enticing employment packages to attract bright, motivated graduates. Furthermore, the cost of living is likely to be considerably cheaper than you will find in the more popular cities on the coasts where everyone seems to want to live.

Be Ready to Move

If you think you couldn't possibly make a move such as this, consider the fact that you will probably never be more mobile than you are right now. Middle-aged workers with children in school and mortgages to pay are extremely hard-pressed to pull up roots and relocate, but even some of them are doing so in search of better work opportunities. As a young graduate, without a home to sell or family obligations to interfere with an interstate move, you have a big advantage over these older cohorts.

You should investigate all the opportunities available to you in faster-growing parts of the country. Remember, as well, that the salary you earn now is likely to influence the future salaries you will be able to command. A move to a different part of the country doesn't have to be permanent, but it can be a great way to jump-start a stalled career while you wait for the rest of the national economy to recover. When you return, you will have enhanced job skills and an enriched job history to report on your updated resume.

TURNING YOUR SURVIVAL JOB INTO YOUR DREAM CAREER

In Chapter 2, I discussed how a ship at sea during a sudden hurricane seeks "any port in a storm." Taking that idea to heart, you may have found temporary employment refuge in a position that doesn't require a college degree, such as waitressing, bartending, or working in a call center.

First, I want to congratulate you for your willingness to make hard adjustments and adapt to difficult circumstances. That takes guts. I also want to remind you to be grateful for having any job at all. Even if you don't expect to be staying long, you should appreciate and acknowledge the temporary hospitality that this employer is offering you. He probably suspects you won't be staying long, either, so the least you can do is to do a good job while you are there.

But guess what? There may be more opportunity in your current job than you think. Let's say you found a job working at Panera Bread or Starbucks. If you survey the situation carefully, you may notice that you are part of a major business chain with a powerful, recognized brand. Big chains have national and international offices, which require the contributions of qualified and capable executives to propel the business forward. They appreciate the talents of someone who understands every aspect of the business, including the "front line" of dealing directly with the customer, yet is also educated at the college level. If you do a good job and make it your business to learn every aspect of the entire operation, who knows how far you could rise within the organization?

Don't look at the little picture: *I'm a lowly barista serving coffee for minimum wage in my isolated hometown.* Instead, try thinking: *I'm an entry-level employee with advancement potential in a successful multinational corporation. This could be the start of something big!*

Your individual franchise has a supervisor or manager whose duties and responsibilities differ substantially from those of the lowest-paid employees. With hard work and dedication, you may be able to rise to one of those positions. Plus, national chains are always looking to add new franchise locations as they expand and grow. Franchise ownership is a big responsibility, but it can also carry big rewards. Who better to open and run a new location than a college-educated employee who has worked in every aspect of the business, starting at the bottom? Who better to train new employees in their job duties? You could set this as your ultimate career goal.

Opportunities Through Independent Businesses

If you find yourself in more of a Mom-and-Pop operation rather than a national chain, this presents a different set of unique opportunities. Because the business is small, you will have the opportunity to view every aspect of the entire operation close up and you will have direct access to the final decision-makers. If you prove yourself to be trustworthy and reliable, who knows where it may lead? You might be offered significantly increased responsibilities. If not, you may learn, from observation and practice, how to run your own successful business and be a boss someday.

Even the seemingly humblest of occupations can be viewed as the path to creating something magnificent, depending on your attitude toward your work. Have you ever heard the story about the three bricklayers? Once, a passerby saw three men laying bricks. He walked over to the first man and asked, "What are you doing?" The man gruffly answered: "What does it look like I'm doing? I'm laying bricks!" He walked over to the second bricklayer and asked him the same question. The second man said, "Oh, well, I'm just making a living." The passerby then walked over to the third bricklayer and asked him the same question: "What are you doing?" The third man looked up, smiled broadly, and said, "I'm building a great cathedral!"

What are you doing? Are you just laying bricks, or are you building a great cathedral as you go through the daily routine of earning a living? The answer depends on your perspective. Every performer is taught that "there are no small roles, only small actors." Well, it is the same with jobs. You can always find meaning and value in your work if you view it correctly and resolve to always give your best performance, no matter what.

I hope you will look at every job you take as a worthwhile learning experience and a path to your highest purpose. View every boss as a future recommendation letter or a positive reference. Even the worst boss can have something valuable to teach you, although the lesson may inadvertently be on how to deal successfully with difficult people.

Strive to be bigger than the job you have and think beyond it to what you could ultimately make of it. Everyone starts somewhere, and usually it's on the bottom. Pay attention to the work your supervisors are doing and educate yourself about the company, its various divisions, and its overall business plan. Be sure to meet and impress the managers in charge and to prepare yourself for advancement opportunities within the organization, while fulfilling and exceeding the obligations of your current position. Companies want to see if you'll hang in there through tough times instead of getting discouraged and giving up. Show them that you are the type of employee with staying power and promotion potential. This is the path to success.

FINDING CREATIVE OUTLETS

It is possible that, even with a great attitude and hard work, your "day job" simply cannot satisfy your true calling. Perhaps you planned to become a stockbroker, an artist, or an architect, but you haven't found work in your desired field yet. In this case, it makes perfect sense to seek out a survival job that is flexible enough to allow you to pursue your passions during your off time.

For ages, newcomers striving to break into competitive fields such as acting, music, or screenwriting have found themselves waiting tables by night while attending auditions or penning their screenplays during the day, or vice versa. Even if they don't find slinging hash particularly fulfilling, there is nobility in the struggle to achieve their dreams, and this work fits into the bigger plan. These days, aspiring financial planners, teachers, and other trained professionals may need to work other jobs, while keeping their eyes firmly fixed on the professional prize they are seeking.

If you need to take survival work in one field while planning a career in another, find ways to stay involved and intellectually engaged with your profession of choice. There are many ways you can do this.

- You can join and attend annual meetings of the professional organizations in your field. This will allow you to continue networking, which could prove the ticket to getting an entry-level job in your career area. You should remain up-to-date with the latest developments in your field by reading the trade or professional journals regularly.

- You can pursue aspects of your preferred career as a freelancer.

- You can seek an internship or informational interviews with a desirable organization that is not currently hiring.

- You can join or create a club centered around your professional interest, which will make a nice addition to your resume.

- You can also make progress toward advanced training or licensure, if relevant.

- You can start a related side business after hours, which might someday become your primary occupation.

A BALANCED LIFE

There are many facets to living a full and balanced life, and a job is just one of these. You should also maintain a healthy range of personal interests and a full social calendar. Don't allow your difficulties in finding ideal work keep you from maximizing other important aspects of your life. For instance, personal coaches will tell you that you should develop yourself in a range of different areas, such as:

- **Physical**

- **Career**

- **Money**

- **Health**

- **Friends/Family**

- **Romance**

- **Personal Growth**

- **Fun and Recreation**

Take a moment right now and give yourself a satisfaction ranking from 1 to 10 in each of these eight areas (1 being "no satisfaction," 5 being "moderately satisfied," and 10 being "total satisfaction"). Of course, it would be unrealistic for anyone to score a 10 in all of these areas, but it is reasonable to expect to score better than a forty (a 5 in each category) when you add them all up. This means that if your Career and Money scores are coming in around a 1 or a 2, then you need to be compensating for that by increasing your satisfaction in other areas of your life.

If your job is currently not your main creative outlet, you may wish to focus on building your physical fitness, learning a new language, or improving your love life. You may decide to become more involved with a religious organization or to coach a youth sports team. Later, when your career hits full stride, you may have to shift your priorities and you might not have time to pursue some of those activities anymore. Then, while your career satisfaction may rise, your fulfillment in other areas of your life may decline. So don't waste this career lull sitting around feeling sorry for yourself; even if certain career paths are currently closed to you, many avenues of personal development remain open and you may soon be wishing you had used this interlude in your life more wisely when your career finally does take off. Make the most of the time available to you and keep moving forward in whatever directions are available.

Look at the Bigger Picture

Just because your career is stuck in low gear does not mean that your entire life is in the doldrums. On the contrary: you now have the extraordinary opportunity to recognize, from a young age, that work isn't everything. Having faced trouble getting launched into your first career, you are unlikely to build your entire self-concept around your job. This experience is likely to leave a lasting mark on your generation, and it may ultimately prove to be a positive impact.

Previous generations were often herded straight from school into predictable, stable careers for the next thirty years without pause, until they could collect their "gold watches" upon retirement. It was a familiar story that some of those workers passed away shortly after they retired, and the explanation given was often that the new retiree was "lost" without his work, because it had consumed his entire life and constituted his entire identity.

A job should *never* constitute your entire identity. I hope you will look upon this unexpected interruption in your work life as an opportunity to reflect upon your life goals and to find broader meaning in your life. You may develop into a much more well-rounded individual as a result.

LEARNING FROM YOUR ELDERS

Speaking of previous generations, understanding them better may assist you in finding your first job and getting promoted. Currently, there are four distinct generations in the workforce: the Traditional Generation, Baby Boomers, Generation X, and Generation Y/Millennials. Each was shaped, for better or for worse, by different historical forces and each brings different values and expectations to the table. As the "new kid" on the block, you are going to have to get along with the older generations on the job.

Even though you might not share their views, life experiences, or perspectives, you should demonstrate respect for their hard-earned experience and try to learn as much as you can from them. This is simply good manners, but it is also to your competitive advantage. The older generations in the workforce have traditionally viewed the latest younger generation with a certain amount of skepticism and complained about their poor work ethic, so don't be surprised to encounter this attitude as a new, young employee, and be prepared to disprove it.

Each generation has its own particular identity.

The Traditional Generation grew up during World War II, and many of them served in the military; they believe strongly in values like sacrifice and patriotism. They like when the work world is structured with clear ranks and hierarchies. This generation tended to stay in one town or with one employer for an entire lifetime and career. These workers now comprise a small minority of the workforce and they will all be retired soon, but their attitudes left a big impression on the structure of organizations.

The Baby Boomers are the most numerous members of the workforce. When they first began working, they had to follow the rules established by their managers from the WWII generation in order to succeed. So, Boomers tend to have a lot in common with them because they adopted many of their values. Because Boomers, by virtue of their sheer numbers, faced plentiful competition from one another, they learned to put in very long hours to "get ahead" of their peers. Boomers, by and large, are known for putting their work ahead of their personal lives and they tend to expect the same of others.

Next came **Generation X**. Just like you, they entered the workforce during a major recession and had trouble finding good jobs right out of college. Because they followed the Boomers, members of Generation X quickly recognized that their career progress was going to be stalled for decades by the "gray ceiling" of older, more experienced, and more numerous workers ahead of them. Hence, many Gen Xers chose to start their own businesses in response to their limited traditional job opportunities. They learned to adapt, innovate, and seek nontraditional career paths. Many also sought to lead more "balanced" work lives than their Boomer predecessors and insisted on more family-friendly workplace policies. If they weren't going to have the same swift career advancement as their predecessors, many Gen Xers reasoned that it made sense to invest some of their energy in other aspects of their lives.

Some members of the older generations labeled them "slackers" unwilling to "pay their dues." However, Gen Xers eagerly seized upon the computer revolution and quickly learned the new technology. Members of this generation were the original computer *wünderkinds*, and helped to develop the Internet. Their computer savvy meant that, for the first time ever, the younger employees in the workforce had to teach the older employees how to handle technology at work. This made them extremely valuable in the workplace.

The youngest generation in the workforce is **Generation Y** (right after X)—sometimes called the Millennials or the Baby Boomlet, since their parents were likely Boomers. That's you! Gen Y shares many of the same traits as Gen X, but to an even greater degree. Y is the first generation that always had a computer. You are accustomed to staying in touch constantly through cellphones—something previous generations lacked. Unlike older generations, which prized conformity, Gen Y likes to personalize everything and to share their opinions on every subject on blogs, Facebook, and social networking websites. (Incidentally, don't be surprised if one of your first job assignments is to help develop or improve your employer's social networking strategy. If they don't ask: offer. This can be a great way to gain recognition and prove your worth by adding value to your employer's bottom line.)

Now, you may not like hearing this part, but listen anyway. Many older workers view members of your generation as being spoiled and coddled. Some have complained that Gen Yers have an "entitlement mentality," which means expecting to get something for doing nothing—or very little. They think your generation received prizes for every small accomplishment, whether it was good or not. Some believe that Gen Y's social skills are lacking, due to too much independent "screen time" spent in front of computers or video games during childhood.

Now that you know what the stereotype of your generation is, resolve to defy it. Show them that you are different! Demonstrate to your work superiors that you appreciate their struggles and respect their values, rather than expecting them to adopt yours. This attitude can really take you places and impress the people with the power to hire and promote you.

Currently, Baby Boomers make up nearly half of the entire workforce, but that's going to change dramatically as the oldest Boomers finally begin to retire. The "gray ceiling" that is holding younger workers back is just beginning to show some cracks and let some light through, which is great news for you and for the ever-patient Gen Xers. Together, the next two younger generations combined (Gen X and Y/Millennials) are almost as numerous as the Boomers. Nevertheless, you can expect that Boomer values will continue to dominate in the workplace for a while longer, so be prepared to adapt to them.

The key to succeeding in an intergenerational workplace is understanding where the other generations are coming from. You will have to exhibit patience and pay some dues, as older employees had to do before you. You should remain optimistic, however, for as the Baby Boomers retire, you can expect to see rapid opportunities for advancement. Just be mindful of the fact that Generation X has been paying an awful lot of dues and waiting patiently for their turn since long before you arrived on the work scene.

Resolve to learn everything you can from the older generations on your first job. They have much to teach you! You may find that older supervisors do not expect to hear much from younger employees at the lower end of the organizational hierarchy. Some older managers don't think they should have to explain things to new employees. They may expect you to figure things out on your own. Others will try to micromanage your every move. Don't be afraid to speak up when you need more explanation, but be careful not to badger your boss with constant e-mails or questions. Older managers may not appreciate it, and they may come to the conclusion that you aren't too bright if you do so. So, learn to read your boss's signs and adapt your behavior to what is expected of you, just as you learned to adjust to different teachers and professors in school.

FINDING INSPIRATION FOR THE LONG JOURNEY

I can't emphasize enough the importance of training yourself in the right mental attitude to find lasting career success. Being unemployed is very disheartening—especially for an eager new college graduate—and making do with a less-than-optimal job can be very discouraging. It can be hard to maintain your optimism in the face of difficult employment odds during a poor economy, especially when you are just starting out. Therefore, I want to offer you some recommendations on famous, classic motivational books that will help you find the inspiration you need to persevere. These books have helped many generations face and overcome tremendous challenges and achieve great success despite them. They will help you, too.

How to Win Friends and Influence People

This book by Dale Carnegie will help you develop the people skills that can lead to lasting success. This classic book has been in print for many years and you should easily be able to pick up a cheap used copy. If you follow the advice in this book, you will develop into the kind of individual who can inspire and motivate others. You will be welcome and warmly regarded in any workplace, and other people will want to help you succeed and achieve your goals.

Think and Grow Rich

This book by Napoleon Hill is considered by many to be the "Granddaddy of All Motivational Literature." In it, Hill outlines his wise "Laws of Success," which took him a lifetime to formulate. Because it was published in 1937, it is now in the public domain, which means you ought to be able to find a free copy to download on the Internet. Try here: *www.think-and-grow-rich-ebook.com.*

As a Man Thinketh

Written by James Allen, this book will help you enlarge your way of thinking. This work is also now in the public domain. If you visit *www.asamanthinketh.net*, you will be able to download a free e-book version and also access works by other inspirational thinkers such as Jim Rohn, Zig Ziglar, and Dr. Wayne Dyer. (You can also purchase a paper copy, published by Adams Media.)

I would also recommend that you check out *The Road Less Traveled* by M. Scott Peck, which will help you on your path to self-discovery. *The 7 Habits of Highly Effective People* by Stephen Covey will help you be more efficient and show you other strategies for getting ahead. More recently, many have enjoyed *The Secret*, which is built around the idea of the Law of Attraction. Essentially, this means that if you put positive energy out into the world, then you will receive positive returns. You can probably pick up used copies of this book at affordable prices or you can learn more at *www.thesecret.tv*.

Once you experience the morale boost you can gain from reading motivational literature, you will discover your favorite writers and turn to them again and again for advice and replenishment. You can benefit greatly from the wisdom of all of these authors and learn to assimilate their skills. I hope you will make a lifetime habit of reading positive, motivational literature to maintain your enthusiasm and help you identify and reach your long-term goals. It is hard enough to stay inspired when the economy is going strong, but when you are facing unemployment or under-employment, you need an extra dose of encouragement.

You may need to adjust your short-term strategies to match the job market, but you should not scale back your long-term plans. Go for what you really want in life! Don't let a recession stop you or cause you to lower your expectations. Richard Bach, another inspirational writer, offers this advice: "You are never given a dream without also being given the power to make it true." Then he added this crucial reminder: "You may have to work for it, however."

As long as you remain willing to work hard, and are adaptable, you will still be able to reach your career goals. Your time frame for achievement may need to be adjusted, but your aspirations can remain the same.

HIRE YOURSELF

There may come a time when you decide that the best way to improve your employment circumstances is to "take matters into your own hands." Despite your best efforts, you may find yourself working in a dead-end job with no advancement potential. Or, despite sending out hundreds or even thousands of resumes, and filling out countless job applications, you may still find yourself without any job at all. In other words, you're drowning and you can't find *any* available port in the storm.

What do you do in this situation? That's easy. You build a life raft. One way of constructing an effective lifesaver is to "hire yourself" by starting your own business. In other words, when life hands you lemons . . . open a lemonade stand!

Being unemployed for a long period of time can be very disheartening, but you are very lucky. You live in a time when you never have to be unemployed or rely on a job offer to ensure that you have productive work to do. Thanks to the Internet, for virtually no start-up cost, you always have the capacity to start your own business and take it, literally, worldwide. You can advertise online and reach thousands of potential customers using nothing but your own ingenuity. Compare this to previous generations, which had no communication means to reach distant customers—who in turn were reliant on big corporations to provide them with access to products. It's actually a great time to be unemployed. If you are creative and disciplined, you can make your own opportunities from thin, wireless air.

You may never have planned on becoming a business owner, but there can be plenty of rewards for doing so—from tax advantages to flexibility and the chance to be your own boss. Many displaced middle-aged workers, tired of leaving their career prospects in the hands of others, have successfully started their own businesses. This strategy also worked quite successfully for many members of Generation X, who themselves faced a cool reception to the working world.

According to reports by Yahoo! Finance, entrepreneurship is currently at a fifteen-year high. This is mainly due to the difficult hiring climate caused by the global recession. As the old saying goes, necessity is the mother of invention. When you need a job but can't find one, you can always make your own. Some people become "accidental" business owners because they can't find a job, but ultimately decide that it was the best thing that ever happened to them. Business owners get to call all the shots. They also get to shoulder all the responsibilities and reap all the rewards that come from owning a business.

What *Sort* of Business?

Even if you ultimately decide not to start a business, going through the decision-making process forces you to grapple with some very important issues.

■ **What sorts of businesses have the best chance of success in this economy?**

■ **How do you keep costs low and productivity high, so as to earn a profit?**

■ **How do you motivate yourself to show up every day and work hard, without someone else to hold you accountable?**

■ **How would you satisfy your customers and what would they expect from you?**

■ **What do you do about taxes and protecting your business from potential liability with insurance?**

All of these questions will help you understand the challenges every business faces and make you a better, more informed, and more proactive employee, should you ultimately choose to work for someone else.

Look for Resources

If you think that launching a business might be right for you, take advantage of all the resources available to help you. First, speak with family members and any business owners you know. Ask them for their advice or if they might be interested in starting a business with you.

I recommend that you contact SCORE, the Service Corps of Retired Executives. This national organization offers free small business advice to aspiring entrepreneurs. They offer counseling, in person or by phone/e-mail, and the opportunity to be assigned to an experienced, individual mentor in your specific business field.

SCORE can help you write a business plan, develop a marketing strategy, and learn many other essential facets of business management. They offer low-cost workshops on virtually every aspect of business development. These can be great places to connect with other business people and exchange ideas. SCORE is a resource partner with the U.S. Small Business Administration and has 364 chapters nationwide. To learn more about their services, visit *www.score.org*.

The Kauffman Foundation is another organization devoted to promoting entrepreneurship; they offer useful resources for small business builders at *www.kauffman.org*. Your local Chamber of Commerce may also be a good source of business advice, so be sure to look into their offerings, as well.

You can discover a great business idea almost anywhere. The essential principle is this: you recognize an existing need and then find a way to fill it. For instance, I noticed that there are a lot of unemployed college graduates in the world and I saw that there was a growing need for helpful information and support. I spotted an opportunity to fill this need, and so I was inspired to write this book to assist people in this situation. The book is my business.

Some businesses require a great deal of monetary capital to start, but others, like this book, merely require time and effort. According to Mike Michalowicz, author of *The Toilet Paper Entrepreneur*, many lucrative businesses can be started for under $5,000. He believes that lack of money can actually be a competitive advantage, since it forces you to develop a streamlined, smarter business approach. He offers several affordable moneymaking recommendations, including consulting, app development, and vending machines, along with implementation ideas and inspirational success stories. If you haven't found a job, then you probably have extra time on your hands. Put on your thinking cap and try to figure out an existing need that you could fill better than existing competitors in the marketplace. Once you have your idea, the hard work will be easy, because you will be excited about making your vision a reality.

ENTREPRENEURIAL IMMORTALITY

Listening to the biography of the late Steve Jobs reminded me of one of the most exciting reasons to start a business of your own: a business can outlive you. Jobs was obviously intensely focused on creating great products, but he was equally concerned with creating an amazing organization that would continue to be able to produce wonderful products in perpetuity. Corporations, unlike people, can last indefinitely and be passed on as a legacy to our children and grandchildren. College degrees, unfortunately, cannot.

I happen to live in a community with large numbers of Amish and Mennonite families who eschew higher education and instead focus their attention on starting and maintaining family businesses. Without assuming the considerable expense of college, they invest their economic resources in their businesses. In doing so, they are frequently able to provide jobs to their immediate family members and even extended relatives and friends. They continue to thrive financially, even in the midst of economic recession, and I can see the wisdom behind their time-proven choices and philosophy, even though it differs from the path followed by the majority of society. My point, here, is that most college students do not receive strong encouragement to start businesses. College tends to prepare students to become employees rather than entrepreneurs—and that even includes most college business programs! But, business formation offers many advantages worth serious exploration and consideration. Remember: the free enterprise system is always open for business and is always hiring.

Pooling Talent with Family and Friends

When you consider the resources available to you as a budding entrepreneur, don't overlook the obvious. You have friends and family—why not consider combining your mental resources and talents to come up with a solution to your unemployment problem and invent ways for you all to earn some money? If you know other unemployed people who are college graduates like you, then surely they bring a variety of knowledge and abilities to the table.

You may discover that you have a very talented pool of human resources from which to draw and potentially launch and grow a business. Assess the skills of those in your immediate circle of influence. You probably already know several intelligent people with a variety of talents who could serve different roles in a fledgling business organization. If no one else is taking a chance on hiring you, why not hire yourselves? Together, you could conceivably launch an enterprise and spend your time together working to build a successful organization that you would own and control. You just need to come up with a good idea and a coherent business/marketing plan to promote it.

This is what a job-seeking group of young graduates from Sarah Lawrence College did. Rather than competing against one another for a limited number of job openings within the media field, these alumni decided to join forces to jumpstart their careers. The result is the Meerkat Media Collective, a collaborative, full-service film production company that has been able to create opportunities for members that they might not have been able to land independently. Meerkat Media uses a "cooperative model" to employ the skills of filmmakers, musicians, teachers, writers, designers, and actors in completing projects for companies such as HBO, MTV, Penguin Books, and Google. You can learn more about their innovative approach at *www.meerkatmedia.org*.

Recessions often spur entrepreneurial activity, as traditional job opportunities dry up. A stalled economy is a great time to undertake a business start-up. Here is a short list of famous businesses that launched during an economic recession:

- **IBM**

- **Hewlett Packard**

- **Disney**

- **MTV**

- **Trader Joe's**

- **FedEx**

- **CNN**

- **Supercuts**

- **Industrial Light & Magic**

- **Microsoft**

Your family also has a vested interest in seeing you succeed. There may be relatives in your family who own their own businesses and who are looking for a helping hand. Older family members may be looking to retire and need someone to help run the business or to take over. If not, perhaps other members of your family might be interested in "going in" on a new business venture with you. You might be able to find family members willing

to finance some of your start-up costs. Since time imme-
morial, families have started businesses as a means of
providing ongoing employment and income to future generations. Drive down the commercial streets in your town
and pay attention to the numbers of small, independent
businesses that you see. Each one required a bold risk-
taker to open its doors. That could be you.

These days, many unemployed college graduates also
have parents or other older relatives who have lost their
long-term jobs, and may feel that they are "too old" to find a
new position at the same level. This may be an opportunity
to partner up with an unemployed relative to start a new
enterprise. You could become the first person in your family to start a business, which might someday employ your
own children so that they will never have to face unemployment the way you did.

Sometimes hardships, like unemployment, provide the
motivation we need to take bold action. This could be the
start of something big; instead of being unemployed, you
could eventually be in a position to employ others. Wouldn't
that be a neat way to turn bad luck inside out?

Starting a business when you're not bringing in a steady
paycheck may seem like a formidable task, but there is a
very good reason why now is a great time for you to consider becoming an entrepreneur: there's a lower opportunity cost to starting a business when you're already
unemployed. When you are employed and want to start
a business, you have to consider giving up the security
offered by the job with a steady paycheck. The fear of giving up a secure income is enough to stop many people from

ever striking out on their own and launching their dream business.

In this economy, when you're unemployed, what have you got to lose by starting a business? You have, ironically, been given the gift of fearlessness. Your worst fear, unemployment, has already materialized and you're still standing. You might as well take your chances and see if you can make a go of your own business enterprise! If you do your research, you may find that your competitors have been significantly weakened during the recession, and their organizations may be too big to enable them to trim costs and adjust course easily. This opens the door for a smarter, more streamlined business to come along and seize market share.

Likewise, the time has probably never been better for acquiring the real estate necessary for operating many businesses. Property prices have fallen dramatically and interest rates on mortgages are at historic lows. There are many affordable foreclosure properties available at bargain basement prices in many regions of the country. This could be a great time to acquire one. Why not begin making inquiries with realtors who specialize in commercial properties to see what is available in your area? You might be pleasantly surprised. And, while it may not seem affordable to you individually, it could possibly be affordable to a small group of investors. Can you pool resources?

In my hometown, there are many older business properties located along the main commercial strip that provide living accommodations upstairs. Some are older homes that were converted into business properties decades ago, but which have fallen into disrepair. It is clear, just from driving by, that the upper living quarters are vacant in several of them. Many of these properties are fixer-uppers—with a little ingenuity and elbow grease, they could really be something! It just takes a person with vision and determination to find the potential in an overlooked piece of property like that.

You may also be able to find whole businesses for sale, including equipment, at liquidation prices. This can sometimes be a better option than starting from scratch, because you may be able to find a business with an existing customer base and established reputation. You can find out about these opportunities through real estate agents or business brokers.

Obviously, purchasing a property, starting a business, or entering a partnership requires a great deal of thought, planning, and discussion. This is not something to leap into without a great deal of investigation and due diligence, but it is certainly an avenue worth exploring. To learn more about buying or starting a business, I suggest that you begin by exploring the free resources available at the U.S. Small Business Association (*www.SBA.gov*) and *www.Nolo.com*, which offers free legal information.

SHOULD YOU DO AN INTERNSHIP?

If you're desperate to break into a specific, hard-to-crack career field, you might want to consider offering to "work" for free. By this, I mean you may want to offer your services as an intern. Most interns are still students, but increasing numbers of unemployed graduates are now pursuing internships as a means of trying to establish connections and break into an organization. You can, too.

══════BY THE NUMBERS══════

In recent years, the use of interns has exploded. According to the National Association of Colleges and Employers (NACE), back in 1992, just 10 percent of graduating college seniors participated in either a paid or unpaid internship. By 2006, the percentage had jumped to 83 percent—2.5 million U.S. students annually. A separate NACE survey found that three-fourths of employers said that experience from an internship, whether at their workplace or elsewhere, was the "primary" reason for hiring a new worker. If you didn't complete an internship as an undergraduate, you may now be at a competitive disadvantage in the labor pool.

═══════════$═══════════

Internships have long been used as a way for an aspiring employee to get his or her foot in the door of a desired organization. Internships, like entry-level work, can provide ways for people without job experience to learn more about a specific career field, build connections, and develop their skill set. Many internships are unpaid while others offer modest compensation. In essence, an internship allows an employer to "try you out" for free, with no commitment. This is a great deal for a business owner, and few will turn it down. To extend the sport metaphor a bit further, if you have a good try-out, you may earn a spot on the team. According to the most recent internship survey conducted by the National Association of Colleges and Employers, 67 percent of interns were ultimately offered full-time positions.

Interns abound in certain competitive white-collar fields, including investment banking, politics, publishing, and broadcasting. Many of these fields have long traditions of providing interns with valuable training opportunities and business contacts in return for their unpaid (or low-paid) labor. A good internship can also provide you with an impressive business's name and reference to list on your resume.

If you completed an internship during your undergraduate education and made a good impression, you should certainly let those contacts know that you are searching for employment now. If they are not currently in a position to hire you, they may be able to refer you to other organizations with suitable openings.

Finding an Internship

As a college graduate, you may face a hurdle in securing an internship, since most internship programs were created and are operated with college students in mind. Don't worry—this hurdle is surmountable. However, you will have to be proactive and resourceful. You may have to convince a company to create an opening for you. Although this can be intimidating, it is also an excellent way of demonstrating that you know how to take the initiative and create opportunities. Smart employers will respect this.

The first thing to do is target a company for whom you'd like to work. If you already have a contact at the company, you should contact that individual. If not, conduct some simple online research to identify an appropriate contact person within the firm. Send a polite e-mail or place a phone call to request an "informational interview." An informational interview is simply a no-obligation opportunity to sit down with a person and ask questions to learn more about that person's job and the organization. It is a low-pressure encounter, because it is not a formal interview for an existing job opening. Nevertheless, you will want to dress and behave professionally, as though it were a job interview. (Informational interviews are also a great place to practice and polish your interviewing skills.)

At the end of the discussion, you should be more knowledgeable about the firm and its operations. At this point, you may have some ideas of existing projects or divisions that might be of specific interest to you. This would be a good point to ask if there is a way you could arrange an internship with the organization to learn more.

If you have ideas for ways you might be valuable to the organization, by all means say so. Also, stress that you are hardworking, flexible, and eager to learn. If you do not feel comfortable asking for an internship at the end of the interview, thank the person for his or her time, go home and reflect on the encounter, and then, once your ideas are better formed, suggest an internship in a follow-up e-mail or handwritten note. This may lead to the offer of a second chance to sit down and continue the discussion or directly to an internship offer.

Making the Most of an Internship

As an intern, it is essential to approach the opportunity with the right attitude. You have your foot in the door, but the only way to open the door the rest of the way is to excel in your internship. Make yourself as useful as possible. Bring the same level of professionalism to an internship that you would bring to the job if you were hired, and show them what you can really do. Go above and beyond.

Ideally, an internship will be a period of specialized and focused training to upgrade your job skills, after which you will be so valuable to the organization that they may wish to hire you in a permanent capacity or recommend you to colleagues. In return for your hard work, you should be able to learn how a particular business works, while meeting industry insiders. This is precious insight and knowledge, which can be hard to gain any other way.

Remember that your internship supervisors are taking time away from their other responsibilities to share their knowledge and expertise with you, so reward them by making it worth their while. Read up on the industry after hours so that you can reduce the time and energy they will have to spend teaching you the basics. Take every opportunity to lunch with colleagues or network with them after hours, because you never know which contacts may hear of potential employment opportunities for you. If you impress them, they will remember you and even seek you out when full-time openings arise.

Undoubtedly, your generation will be faced with many challenges in trying to find suitable opportunities in the labor market. You may have to swallow some of your pride and prove highly adaptable and flexible to overcome the odds that are currently stacked against you. In such a competitive employment environment, your college degree may not be enough to set you apart from the rest of the job-seeking pool anymore, but the right attitude will. It can always open doors in any economy, and you can take that to the bank.

CHAPTER FIVE

STUDENT LOANS AND HEALTH INSURANCE

There are a lot of four-letter words nobody likes to hear. As an unemployed graduate you may be dealing with one of the most unpleasant: your loan. Two-thirds of bachelor's degree recipients now have student debt. The average college graduate today carries five figures of student debt and some even have debt reaching six figures. Without a job, how on earth are you supposed to pay any of it back?

First of all, if you are completely unemployed with no income, you should look into deferment, forbearance, or other forms of payment relief. According to the Federal Reserve Bank of New York, as many as one in four student borrowers are already behind on their student debt payments. Don't join them! You need to take action to manage your loan responsibility promptly; don't slip into denial and allow the problem to worsen. You need to ask for a deferment while you are still making timely payments. If you ignore your payments, hoping that the problem will simply "go away," you will just incur costly late fees and damage your credit rating, and future options will be closed to you. This will merely compound your challenges. Don't run away from the problem. Face it head on.

The first step is to contact your lender. You should be able to find this information on your loan documents or you can look it up on the U.S. Department of Education's Student Loan Data System which you can find here: *www.nslds.ed.gov/nslds_SA*. If it is a federal loan, you can also call 1-800-4FEDAID and speak to someone who will help you work out a solution.

Here are some of the options that may be available to you.

DEFERMENT

A deferment is a temporary suspension of loan payments and interest for specific situations, such as unemployment. Some other situations that may make it possible for your loan payments to be deferred include:

- **Economic hardship**

- **Re-enrollment in school**

- **Active duty military**

- **National service**

- **An internship**

- **Other similar situations, on a case-by-case basis**

The only way to find out if you qualify for a deferment is to apply for one and see what happens. Just because you apply for a deferment does not mean you will automatically receive it, so don't make assumptions. It is essential to continue making payments until you are notified that your request for a deferment is granted. This can take a little time, which is why it is so important not to delay your request.

Deferments can be a great relief if you are temporarily unemployed. You should apply as soon as it is clear that you will be unable to keep up with your payments. To apply for a deferment, you must contact your lender directly or you could begin by contacting the financial aid office at your college to ask for their advice.

You don't have to pay interest on the loan during deferment if you have a subsidized loan. If your loan is unsubsidized, however, only the principal is deferred and interest will continue to accrue, so be sure you understand the terms of a deferment before deciding if this is the right option for you and before you agree to any changes in a loan obligation.

FORBEARANCE

If you do not qualify for a deferment, you might qualify for forbearance. This means a temporary postponement or reduction of payments for a period of time because you are experiencing financial difficulty. Unlike deferment, even if your loans are subsidized, interest will continue to accrue and you will be responsible for repaying it. The holder of your loan can grant forbearance for up to twelve months at a time for up to three years. As with a deferment, you have to apply for forbearance to your loan servicer.

Change Your Repayment Plan

If you do not qualify for a deferment or forbearance, it may make sense to switch your repayment plan to one that works better for your current financial situation. There are several repayment options available to federal borrowers. Unless you specify otherwise, you will be placed in the standard repayment plan, which means you will be expected to repay your loan in ten years. That can mean a pretty high monthly payment. This is not the only option available to you, however. You could select an extended repayment plan that offers lower monthly payments over a longer period of time (up to twenty-five years). This might result in a larger final pay-off amount, but it could make your payments much more manageable in the short term. To make the switch, you will need to take the initiative by contacting your lender.

The "Pay As You Earn" Plan

The federal government has taken notice of the tremendous burden many new graduates are experiencing as they face both high unemployment and large student loan burdens. To assist, the government authorized easier repayment options to help some strapped borrowers. The purpose of these options is to make your student loan payments more affordable by capping your monthly payment based on your income. This program is intended for borrowers who have high debt compared to their income.

Sometimes these options are called "Income-Based Repayment" or "Income-Contingent Repayment," but the most-used term is "Pay As You Earn." The Pay As You Earn program allows college graduates to cap their federal student loan repayments at 10 percent of their discretionary income (it used to be 15 percent). This reduction allows some borrowers to lower their payments by as much as a few hundred dollars each month. After twenty years, all remaining debt on the federal loans is forgiven. In addition, if you have more than one federal student loan you may be able to consolidate the debt, which could reduce your interest payment.

You have to meet certain requirements for this repayment program. There is a formula that determines whether or not you are eligible for Income-Based Repayment (IBR). To find out whether or not you qualify, visit *www.student aid.ed.gov* and search for the IBR calculator. You can also review all of your other loan options at this website and find out how to request deferments or to change your repayment plan. Remember: Pay As You Earn/IBR *only* applies to federal loans. Private loans are another matter and you will have to discuss the terms of those with your private lender.

Avoiding Delinquency and Default

Student loan default rates have risen sharply in the past few years and federal default rates are the highest they've been in a decade. Data available from the U.S. Department of Education show that default rates are (as of 2012) running at 8.8 percent, which is high. This isn't surprising; naturally, there is a strong relationship between default rates and unemployment rates. A study by the Institute for Higher Education Policy found that for every borrower who defaults, at least two more have fallen behind in making their payments.

With so many people falling delinquent or going into default on their student loans, it's important to understand your options and take charge of your personal loan obligation. One thing to bear in mind is that you will forfeit your right to take advantage of deferment, forbearance, or Income-Based Repayment if you allow your loan to slip into default. This is why it is so important to be responsible about managing your loans.

There can be some very unpleasant consequences if you become delinquent or default on your student loan.

First of all, here's how your loan works: after you graduate, you have a six-month grace period before you have to start repaying your student loan. If you do nothing, you will be entered into the "standard repayment" plan, which means you will be expected to pay back the entire loan in ten years. Your first payment is due the seventh month. If you don't make a payment at that point, your loan will be considered "delinquent" and you will start receiving urgent letters.

After sixty days of delinquency, really unpleasant things can start to happen to you. The lenders will report your late payment to the credit bureaus and lower your credit score. This will probably make it difficult for you to buy a car or a house later on. Even worse, many employers now check the credit reports of applicants, and they are probably not going to be interested in a candidate with a bad credit rating . . . so, ironically, failing to pay your student loan can actually keep you from getting the job that would enable you to pay your loan! This is a bad spiral you want to avoid.

After nine months of delinquency, your loan is considered in "default." At this point, you will no longer qualify for preferential repayment plans. To get out of default, you may have to pay costly collection fees. These can really add up. Also, a portion of your wages or income tax refunds could be taken to help satisfy the debt.

This is not a time to go into denial. You signed a deal to repay this money when you borrowed it, so you have a moral obligation to repay it. If you are in a financial bind due to unemployment, contact your lender, explain your situation, and discuss your options. They would rather work out a satisfactory plan of reduced payments than have you give up on trying to pay it. The sooner you act to avoid or repair default, the better it is for you. Pick up the phone and start the conversation. You can also find very good information about avoiding default and how to manage your student loan obligation on *www.finaid.org* or at *www.studentaid.ed.gov*.

Loan Forgiveness As a Bonus

If your student loans are a big concern for you, you should be aware of the favorable repayment terms offered to borrowers who choose to work in certain fields that the government considers to be in the "public service." This broad category includes more jobs than you may expect, such as emergency management, public safety, healthcare support occupations, early childhood education, assisting the elderly or disabled, public librarians, and work for certain tax-exempt organizations. Even working in a licensed childcare facility may count! After a period of time paying your federal student loan and working full-time in a qualified position, you may be eligible for forgiveness of your remaining loan interest and principal. Depending on your loan circumstances, this opportunity could prove very valuable and might make working in one of these fields a great deal for you. It could cause you to broaden your definition of a "good job" and encourage you to seriously consider fields you may be overlooking. To learn more about the terms, restrictions, and potential benefits attached to these types of jobs, check out the government's own website at: *www.studentaid.ed.gov* and click on "Public Service Loan Forgiveness" or visit *www.finaid.org/loans/publicservice.phtml.* This is a fairly new program, and the first cancellations of loan balances are not due to be granted until 2017, so few people are aware of the magnitude of this opportunity.

Bear in mind that Income-Contingent Repayment and public service loan forgiveness are only available to holders of federal student loans; neither of these new programs applies to holders of private loans made by banks or other lenders.

HEALTH INSURANCE

When you're young and unemployed, it can be pretty tempting to skip health insurance payments. After all, you're already having enough trouble paying your basic living expenses as it is! If you're feeling healthy, then health insurance is probably one of the last things on your mind. It's not surprising, then, that people between ages nineteen and twenty-nine are the most uninsured age demographic in America. The rate of young adults without coverage is nearly double the national average. A lot of young adults figure: what could possibly go wrong if I skip out on health insurance for a few months . . . or years?

The answer, of course, is plenty. The most obvious thing that could go wrong is that you could have an accident. No one ever plans to have one of those, but the reality is that young adults have higher accident rates than those of most other age groups. Then, there is also the slim chance that you could be unexpectedly diagnosed with a costly illness that you couldn't possibly afford to treat without health insurance coverage, such as cancer or diabetes. Without coverage, you might be denied the level of care you need. You need to protect yourself against that.

Ah, the joys of adulthood. The fact of the matter is that health insurance is a necessary and important expense and going without it is simply not a responsible option, even though it may be very tempting. As it so happens, the American health-care system is in a state of major transition right now—just like the rest of the economy. Fortunately, however, there are changes underway that are creating new options that should make it easier and more affordable for you to find insurance, even if you are currently unemployed.

Getting Health Insurance Through Your Parents

Growing up, you probably didn't know what health insurance was and didn't realize your parents were providing it for you. As a minor, your parents' health-care plan covered you, but once you reached age eighteen, the rules changed. After that point, in most cases, your parents' health insurance plan could drop your coverage as a dependent, leaving you to go out and purchase your own. You might not have realized this, because most insurance plans provide an exception for children over the age of eighteen who enroll in college. These children can remain on their parents' health insurance plans until they graduate.

If you went straight from high school to college, you probably never had a break in your insurance coverage. Now may be the first time in your adult life that you have needed to acquire health insurance. It often comes as quite a rude awakening after graduation! Furthermore, the way the health insurance industry is structured in the United States, most people receive health insurance coverage as a benefit from their employers. For better or for worse, this is the way it has traditionally been done. Things seem to be changing, however.

Congress passed a new health-care act that has a number of provisions that may apply to you and your situation. One part of the law was designed with you in mind. It's known as "Dependent–26 Coverage for Young Adults" and it aims to help more young people obtain or keep health insurance. Under this portion of the law, with limited exceptions, private insurance companies that provide coverage to children under their parents' health plans are now required to let young adults stay on those plans up to age twenty-six. Since this provision of the new law was enacted, millions of young adults have gained health insurance coverage this way. You can stay on, or join, an insured parent's health plan whether you are:

- **Single or married**

- **Living with your parents or on your own**

- **In school or out of school**

- **Financially dependent on your parents or completely independent**

Of course, this won't help you if your parents don't have health insurance coverage to extend to you. Also, your parents get to decide if they want to keep you on their health insurance plan, so it helps to maintain a good relationship with them. Dependent–26 coverage is probably the most affordable way for you to receive health insurance, although it may not be free. Your parents will have to make the arrangements to keep you on their insurance plan, so you will have to talk to them about it. They will probably have to pay an additional premium to keep you on their plan, so you should also have a discussion with them about the cost of this and whether you will be expected to contribute to covering some of the extra charges.

Other Options

If you are unable to receive health insurance from your parents, and you do not have a job that offers health insurance, then you are going to have to find a low-cost way to insure yourself. Under the Affordable Health Care Act, being without health insurance is illegal and you could be fined if you fail to obtain any coverage. Therefore, you have to acquire at least minimal health-care insurance. Going without it is simply not a credible option.

Buying health insurance doesn't have to be a major ordeal, nor does it have to be prohibitively expensive. All you need is a bare-bones plan; you don't need high-end, "Cadillac" insurance. Don't confuse health insurance with health care. Health insurance is a way of managing risk; it is not meant to cover every doctor's visit and every pill you might ever need. It is there in case you are struck with a costly health-related expense that could not be antici-pated—kind of like an unexpected car accident.

To extend this metaphor a bit further, think of insuring your body like you insure a car. You don't buy car insur-ance that pays for every car wash, oil change, or minor repair. That would cost a fortune and be completely unnec-essary. Instead, you buy car insurance to cover you in case you accidentally throw the car into drive instead of reverse and plow through the front entrance of a 7–11 store. It's for when you total the car, damage other people's property, or injure someone—not for every minor ding in the door. If you don't have a lot of money to spend on car insurance, then you buy insurance with a high deductible, and you drive very carefully because you know your insurance isn't going to cover every little fender-bender.

Similarly, high-deductible, low-cost health insurance won't pay for every trip to the doctor or every prescription medication you get, but it will kick in if you are suddenly hit with very costly expenses, such as a major operation or a lengthy recuperation from a devastating injury. If you truly are young and healthy, that's all you need. This kind of insurance is sometimes called "Catastrophic Care" because its main purpose is to protect you in case you encounter a medical catastrophe or other health-related emergency. Then, you take good care of your health to minimize your daily out-of-pocket health-care costs, but you can rest assured that you are covered in the event that something major happens.

Finding Low-Cost Health Insurance

Most health insurance companies offer many different plans to fit all budgets, so you could start by identifying a possible insurance company, calling them up, and having a discussion with their representatives. You may be able to purchase your own individual health insurance policy for as low as $25 a month. Young people tend to receive lower rates because they are typically healthy with few chronic illnesses. You could begin your search by going to a website that helps you compare the rates of several insurance companies, such as *www.pennyhealthinsurance.com*, *www.ehealthinsurance.com*, or *www.vimo.com*. If you go back to school, even part-time, you may qualify for low-cost insurance through the college or university, so be sure to investigate that option.

What if you have looked into all the options and still can't find coverage you can afford? Well, according to an Associated Press article titled, "Healthcare options for the young, healthy and broke," which analyzed the complicated provisions of the new health-care law, starting in 2014 you may qualify for help paying for your insurance premiums, dependent on your income. If your income is up to four times the poverty level—that's currently about $44,000 for an individual, then you may be eligible for financial assistance in purchasing private insurance. Those earning the least are expected to pay no more than 2 percent of their incomes toward insurance premiums. According to estimates from the Kaiser Family Foundation, a single adult earning $16,000 would pay roughly $540 annually for coverage, with the rest of the premium being covered by a $2,800 tax credit. The

Kaiser Foundation's website (*www.healthreform.kff.org*) even offers a Health Reform Subsidy Calculator so that you can get a better personal estimate.

You might find that you will soon qualify for low- or no-cost Medicaid coverage. The new health-care law encourages states to expand Medicaid to include adults with incomes up to around $15,000, so this is another possibility to investigate. There are eligibility requirements for Medicaid, which vary from state to state. To learn more, you would need to contact your local Medicaid office. To find them, Google "Medicaid Office" and then your state's name.

You might even decide simply to pay the fine for neglecting to comply with the new insurance requirement; this tax penalty starts as low as $95 annually, depending on income, which would be less than paying premiums, but is expected to rise over time. However, if it would cost you more than 8 percent of your income to buy basic insurance, then you would be exempt from the penalty. Because the new regulations will require insurance companies to accept new customers regardless of any preexisting conditions, some people may decide simply to pay the fine and wait until something happens to seek out coverage. It's not ideal, but that is the way the law is written.

You can stay abreast of the latest news pertaining to health-care regulations by visiting *www.healthcare .gov*. This government website is managed by the U.S. Department of Health & Human Services and includes specific sections that address the Affordable Health Care Act, and it also discusses "The Health Care Law and You." It allows you to review every plan sold in your state to locate the right one for you.

The unfortunate reality is that young adults are traditionally one of the least-insured age groups. Because many entry-level positions lack health coverage, and because young adults tend to earn lower salaries and feel physically healthy (even invincible), the rate of young adults without health coverage stubbornly tends to be much higher than that of the national average. Since the implementation of Dependent–26 care, however, more than 6 million young Americans have picked up coverage through their parents' policies. This is a very positive trend. By staying up-to-date on new insurance options, you should be able to find a level of coverage to protect you that works within your budget.

Many aspects of the economy appear to be shifting, and the idea that we obtain our health insurance through our employer may be one of them. In fact, recent polls now show that fewer Americans than ever before now receive their health insurance through their jobs—less than half. This is a big change, and it may be changing the way we think about employment and work benefits as a nation.

It appears that the age of large organizations—where an employer took care of us "for life"—may be drawing to an inevitable close. As pension schemes fail and promises of lifetime employment with a single company fade into distant memory, we may be shifting back into an era of broader self-employment and greater individual responsibility. This doesn't have to be bad news; many of our great-grandparents ran their own farms or operated small cottage industries out of their houses. One of the biggest hurdles to self-employment today, however, can be providing your own health insurance. Many people have pointed out that unfavorable terms for purchasing individual health insurance policies often function to prevent people from trying to start their own businesses, which can stifle the overall economy and reduce employment opportunities for everyone.

The Affordable Health Care Act and its consequences may, hopefully, make it easier to buy your own health insurance rather than relying on a large employer to supply this to you as part of a group benefits package. This could help facilitate entrepreneurship. So, I would encourage you to pay attention and be flexible and open to emerging new options, both in how you will employ yourself and in how you will manage your health-care coverage. Hopefully, some of the disincentives to purchasing individual health insurance, such as higher prices, will be removed, opening the door to easier self-employment options for more people.

Many young Americans are currently frustrated with both their levels of student loan debt and their access to affordable health insurance options. As a result, new advocacy organizations have begun to emerge to attempt to create positive changes. For those struggling with post-higher-education debt, Student Loan Justice is an excellent source of information, support, and grassroots efforts to reform lending practices. You can learn more about them at *www.studentloanjustice.org.*

Another place to connect with others facing similar challenges is Young Invincibles. This organization was initially founded to provide a voice to young Americans in the ongoing health debate, but has expanded to address additional issues of vital concern to this age group, such as higher education, jobs, the economy, and entrepreneurship. Look for them at *www.younginvincibles.org*.

PART III

YOUR SUPPORT NETWORK

Unemployment doesn't just drain your pocketbook; it also saps your self-confidence. Do yourself a favor and reach out to others while you travel this lonely path. You deserve as much practical and emotional support as you can get during your struggle to land satisfactory employment.

Most people remember how hard it was to land their first job and are extremely sympathetic and responsive to earnest requests for assistance from new graduates. Some of the strongest relationships in life are forged and cemented under trying conditions. Believe it or not, you may even look back on this experience fondly, someday, once you are safely on "the other side."

No matter what your current circumstances are, you have many sources of emotional and practical support from which to draw, ranging from family and friends to fellow alumni or new allies you will meet and develop through face-to-face or online networking. You want to build as many bridges over this troubled water as possible.

There is an old saying that your net worth equals your network. The more people who are on your side, the faster you will be able to open temporarily closed doors and see dramatic results in your life. The more people who know you, and think positively of you, the easier it will be for you to mobilize forces on your behalf. Building and growing these sustaining relationships isn't just a job-hunting strategy, however; it's also part of creating a fulfilling and well-rounded life.

CHAPTER SIX

YOU ARE NOT ALONE

Being unemployed can leave you feeling pretty isolated. When you don't have a group of coworkers to hang out with each day, you have more time to sit, brood, and examine your worries and fears. This is particularly true when it seems that everyone else around you has a job.

Economic downturns come in all shapes and sizes. The 2008 Great Recession was deep and broad enough that pretty much everyone knows several other people in the same proverbial boat. You may not like being unemployed or underemployed, but at least you have a lot of companions on your tough journey. It's comforting to know that you're not the only person in this predicament.

This is actually good news and bad news. The bad news is that when there are a lot of unemployed people, the competition for each existing job opening increases. It is going to take some time before so many unemployed people can be absorbed by a struggling economy.

The good news, however, is that there is plentiful support and empathy available to you from other people who know exactly what you are going through and how you feel. By banding together with other fellow sufferers, you can make the unpleasant aspects of unemployment more tolerable and work together to come up with some creative solutions to your mutual problem.

There is strength and hopefully ingenuity in numbers. There is no reason why groups of unemployed college graduates cannot share living accommodations to reduce their monthly expenses, for instance. This is a no-brainer. There are also untapped opportunities for you to pool your mental resources and capabilities to develop new business ventures that may prove more promising than traditional career paths, which can be difficult to enter in a time of economic downturn.

You may have had some bad luck with your timing in trying to enter the workforce during a recession, but you still have a lot going for you. Being young, educated, and unemployed, you have the energy, time, and mental capacity to devote to a moneymaking project of your choosing. These are enormous resources at your disposal that you should not discount or take for granted. Sure, the economy may be in the toilet, but that is a small concern compared to what youth, energy, and intelligence can accomplish!

Your ultimate goal is financial independence, but interdependence can help you achieve it. It's nice to know that you do not have to walk this path alone, and it would be foolish to do so. You have many potential supporters and peers in your corner to help you, and you can cultivate and grow a bigger network by reaching out and looking for more assistance in the right places.

TAPPING INTO THE POWER OF YOUR ALUMNI NETWORK

As an unemployed college graduate, one of the first places you should be turning to for help is your alma mater. You are now a member of an alumni network that quite possibly spans the entire globe. The school that you share can provide a way of breaking the ice and receiving an introduction to older graduates who may be in a position to help you launch your career.

It can be a little bit disorienting to make the transition from "student" to "alumni," and many graduates simply drift away from their colleges after commencement. This leaves the door open for more enthusiastic grads— like you—to get noticed at planned alumni activities. At most schools, only a minority of graduates become actively involved with their alumni associations, but this core group of devoted people can include some of the most school-spirited. They usually feel a vested interest in promoting the school, which means promoting its graduates. This includes you!

If you become a regular attendee at alumni events and show initiative, before you know it, you'll find yourself working on committees (which are almost always begging for help) and getting to know older, well-connected alumni in your local area. Whenever they are searching for volunteers, throw your arm up and say, "I'll do it!"

Working together with fellow alumni on a shared project is a great way to get to know them on a personal level, and it's also a great way to show them what a great job you can do. If they see that you are hardworking, reliable, and full of great ideas, they will want to tell other people and recommend you to their friends, who may know of job openings. This is such an obvious and affordable avenue for increasing your visibility among people with a vested interest in seeing you succeed that you would be foolish not to take full advantage of all the alumni activities going on in your local area. It's even worth traveling to distant events. Alumni activities also tend to be relatively affordable when compared to the cost of other similar social events or networking organizations, and many alumni associations offer discounted membership pricing to recent graduates, so money should not prevent you from becoming involved.

When human resource offices are deluged with applicants, knowing someone on the "inside" can be crucial in making your application stand out from the rest. It is easier for overwhelmed recruiters to reduce their applicant piles to those who "come recommended," and an alumnus may be able to provide you with that crucial endorsement that can lead to an interview.

BY THE NUMBERS

Alumni networking can be very powerful. According to the *University of Chicago News*, 25 percent of the job and internship opportunities for their students came from alumni contacts. The director of their Career Advising and Planning Services says, "Our greatest resource has been our alumni. They know the strength of a University of Chicago education and the difference U of C graduates can make at an organization. They have been phenomenal at giving leads. And when they have been in the position to hire, they have tried to hire U of C students." Ideally, this is how the alumni network should function at every school, with a tight sense of *esprit de corps* and a mutual willingness to work to advance classmates, even if you didn't attend school at the same time. Just remember that it's a two-way street: when you are in a position to hire or recommend someone, you will also be expected to go out of your way to help your fellow alumni.

Check with Alumni Services

Beyond connecting with individuals who regularly show up at planned alumni events, be sure to check with the career office and also with the alumni services office at your school to determine how you can identify other alumni in your local area or in your preferred field of interest and get to know them. You can also try contacting your undergraduate academic department to ask for referrals to graduates in your field of study. Inquire if there are established procedures for reaching out to alumni or other recommendations for how to get their attention and make the most of these connections. In some cases, you may wish to send a general introduction to multiple alumni letting them know about your skills and notifying them that you would welcome news of job openings or internship possibilities. In other cases, you may wish to be more indirect and seek out informational interviews or general career advice, rather than asking about actual job openings.

You should also look into joining the local chapter of your school's alumni association, so that you will be able to take advantage of available opportunities to mingle and network actively with your fellow graduates. Better yet, consider assuming leadership positions, which will increase your visibility within the organization and provide you with extensive opportunities to interact with the membership.

Of course, just having a diploma from the same school may not be enough to convince a fellow alum to recommend you. Your alumni networking will be much more effective when you build genuine relationships that are not centered solely on asking for help with your job search. This means showing up regularly at events, employed or not, and being willing to lend a helping hand to others when you are in a position to do so. Your alumni network provides you with a reason to get together on a casual, informal basis and begin to build these enduring relationships.

It makes perfect sense to reach out to alumni first when seeking a job. Rather than being a "cold call," a contact with an alum means that you already have something in common—your shared school. There is an element of implied trust and understanding between graduates of the same school that can work to your advantage, if you are persistent in developing your alumni networks. This can help you bridge the gap between "stranger" and "worthy of consideration."

In recognition of the hiring crisis, many schools are attempting to assist their newest alumni by increasing their appeals to older alumni to come together to support and hire recent graduates. Alumni will often list internships and job openings at their alma maters first, hoping to attract students to come and work for their organizations. Likewise, if you belonged to any fraternities, sororities, or other social organizations during your time in college, these are additional "warm" contacts who may be extremely willing to go out of their way to assist you in your quest to find suitable employment. Reach out to them, let them know that you are seeking a job, and ask them to let you know of any opportunities or acquaintances who may be interested in learning more about your qualifications. Again, there is an implied reciprocity to this type of connection. Someday, when you are in a position to hire people, you should look out for members of the organizations that looked out for you.

This is a time for alumni to unite and work together to advance your school's success rate by supporting one another in the workforce. Your college's career center also has an important role to play in helping alumni connect with each other and in helping graduates locate job openings.

CONTACT YOUR COLLEGE CAREER PLANNING OFFICE

If you were a typical undergraduate student, you probably didn't spend too much time in the career office. Rutgers University's study of unemployed graduates, titled "Unfulfilled Expectations," found that 38 percent of graduates wish they had started looking for work much sooner, while they were still in college.

It's never too late to begin, however, and you can still take advantage of the resources available to you through your college career center. Years ago, it was unusual for college career centers to service alumni, but that was before career switching became the norm for most workers. In the past few years, colleges have seen career center use by alumni surge, and some have even responded by hiring counselors specifically for assisting alumni or even, in some cases, by building alumni wings.

So, even though you may wish you had started earlier, it is certainly not too late to go online or pick up the phone and find out how your campus career center can help you. The staff may be able to counsel you remotely, or you can make an appointment to go back to campus to speak to a counselor in person and take advantage of the resources and job listings available there. You will probably also be welcome to participate in any upcoming job fairs or other recruiting events, so be sure to ask about those possibilities, as well.

As a graduate, you are entitled to avail yourself of all the career resources that the school offers to undergraduates, and you should be proactive in taking full advantage of all of them. I encourage you to stay in regular contact with the career center and build a personal relationship with a career counselor there until you find a permanent position. Make sure you know how to access all of the job and internship listings that they receive and use their assistance in crafting your resume and writing cover letters for available positions. If they offer any e-mail updates of job listings or recruitment events, sign up for them. This is part of what your tuition went to fund and you deserve to receive this crucial career support.

FAMILY SUPPORT

Every family is different, but for many unemployed college graduates parental support has proven integral to their survival. While this situation may not be what you'd hoped for when you graduated, full of dreams of independence, it is admirable of parents to pitch in and try to help their young adult children economically when they can't find self-supporting work.

Intergenerational care and shared living arrangements within a family are a tradition dating back centuries. It is only relatively recently that it became a standard expectation for each generation to live under a separate roof. Many previous generations grew up with grandparents in the house, and we may be returning to such a lifestyle in this country. In many European nations, the cost of housing and unemployment are so high that it is extremely common for the youngest generation to live at home with their parents for an extended period of time. In Italy, the average age for "leaving the nest" is thirty-six! While this may be extreme, rising interdependence between generations is not necessarily a bad thing and family members should always be invested, and investing, in each other's success.

BY THE NUMBERS

The Rutgers study mentioned earlier found that significant proportions of graduates are receiving financial assistance from parents with their expenses: 32 percent receive assistance with miscellaneous expenses, including phone bills, 29 percent receive housing support, 26 percent receive help paying for food, and 21 percent receive help paying for health care.

$

Of course, moving back home with your family, or relying on them for some financial support, should never be a one-way street. For any form of financial support that you may receive, there are meaningful ways to reciprocate. For instance, even if you are temporarily not making money, there are many ways you can still contribute to running a household and managing expenses. An extra person in the house increases the laundry, cleaning, and shopping responsibilities; you should volunteer to assume some of these duties to relieve other family members. Likewise, some household maintenance tasks, such as yard work or snow removal, may be too physically taxing for older members of the household. If your parents had previously hired a service for this task, you may be able to save them a tidy sum by offering to do these chores yourself. Even feeding and walking the family dog can be a big help and will be greatly appreciated. Find opportunities to be helpful without being asked.

The Rules for Moving Back Home

It's not easy moving back into your childhood home—for you or for your parents. You're used to having a lot of freedom in college and moving back into your parents' house could feel like a big step backward. It doesn't have to be that way, however, as long as you approach it with an appropriate mindset and keep the lines of communication open. Everyone will probably have certain unstated expectations about how this arrangement should operate. You should reflect on your own expectations. For instance, you're probably assuming that you will be able to come and go as you please without telling anyone where you are heading or what time to expect you back. You may expect to be able to eat anything in the refrigerator, and you might be so used to having your mom cook for you and do your laundry that you can't imagine a different arrangement. This may or may not be realistic now.

There's a good bet that without an honest discussion, everyone will lapse into some familiar habits that might not be appropriate anymore. Just because you move back home for a little while to save some money doesn't mean you should fall through a time warp and regress to outgrown high school behavior.

Your parents probably have some expectations of their own. It's hard to say what those expectations might be without asking them, although I'm pretty sure that they won't want to be picking up after you. They may have a time frame in mind for when they would like you to move out. They may expect you to pay some rent or at least contribute monetarily to the utility bill. Every family is different in this regard, so you have to work out a solution that is right for yours.

Your Extended Family

If moving back home with your parents is not an option, perhaps extended family members or even acquaintances would be willing to rent you a room at a very reasonable rate in exchange for some light chores or housekeeping. This can be a mutually beneficial arrangement for everyone involved and may eliminate some of the difficulties that can arise when adult children move back home.

Again, arrangements such as these were quite common in the not-too-distant past. Families with a large house often advertised a "room to let" for an extra person—relative or not—in exchange for taking on a share of the household duties or very reasonable rent. This is a great option for a young person unable to afford a separate apartment yet, and it can also be a lifesaver for a cash-strapped family having trouble paying their bills. The housing crisis, coupled with high unemployment, has left many homeowners in a very precarious economic situation. Having just one extra person paying a small amount of rent each month could mean the difference between survival and foreclosure for a family on the brink of financial disaster. A live-in arrangement could be a happy win-win situation for everyone, and could even lead to lifelong friendships.

Many foreign jobs offer live-in arrangements, but you don't have to travel overseas to find one. Ask around among your relatives and acquaintances to see if anyone you know would be interested in making a little extra money each month or receiving some other form of assistance by allowing you to occupy an unused room in their house.

SUPPORT FROM UNEMPLOYED FRIENDS

You probably already have several unemployed peers; they can form the foundation of your support group. You should stay in touch with these individuals in order to share your progress in finding a job and to seek their ongoing advice and input. Remember: your unemployed friends need your encouragement and companionship as much as you need theirs. By staying in contact with them, you gain much-needed support while greatly expanding your network of contacts.

It is one thing to keep open informal lines to your friends, but it could be even better to "formalize" the relationship by establishing a regular meeting schedule centered around the goal of finding or creating jobs. You may want to consider taking a leadership role in facilitating these discussions, which could help increase your visibility and bring you into contact with an ever-widening group of people. If you really want to step it up a notch, plan topics for each meeting, and invite members of the community to come in and deliver prepared talks on important subjects of shared concern. You can invite bankers, health-insurance representatives, officers from the local Chamber of Commerce, or small business owners to come and deliver presentations to your group; the possibilities are limited only by your imagination.

Some of these discussions could take place online. For example, you can take the initiative to start a Facebook discussion group and send regular updates and notices of upcoming meetings to members. Facebook already offers an "Unemployed College Graduate Support Group," but there is nothing to stop you from starting your own social networking group dedicated to the specific needs of your personal group of friends. This might become a forum for sharing concerns, but it could also become a useful networking tool. Each one of these contacts may eventually become the source of a job lead or a referral to an acquaintance who might be able to help you land an interview or internship that can finally open resistant doors for you.

The next step, beyond corresponding with people electronically or staying in touch over the phone, is to meet face-to-face in order to enjoy one another's company while sharing ideas and brainstorming ways to improve your circumstances. You get a much richer connection when you meet in person rather than by text. There really is nothing better than sharing a cup of coffee at the local diner or coffee shop. (A tip: Groups of successful businesspeople often regularly meet for breakfast in many cities and towns. If you are an early riser, and you can figure out where they hang out in your local area, you may be able to join them. An easy way to start is by going to local hangouts early in the morning, dressed professionally, and paying attention. Ask the waitresses, too. They will know who the well-connected businesspeople are.) Obviously, the Facebook group would provide a convenient way to announce upcoming get-togethers. It is crucial to continue to maintain your social contacts during periods of unemployment; you do not want to "fall off the radar" and become a recluse.

Strengthen Your Networks

Someday, when you are busy in a full-time job or raising a family, it will be easy to let your social contacts dwindle. Now that you find yourself with extra time on your hands, you actually have an enviable chance to make a serious time investment in forging and strengthening all your relationships. Take time to nurture and build these friendships. They may last a lifetime and sustain you through many of life's ups and downs. This is a great way to enrich your life at little to no cost, while possibly laying the foundations of your future social and business network. You never know who is going to turn out to be a future employer, employee, coworker, or potential buyer, so take the time to build lasting connections that you will maintain even when you reenter the workforce full-time. But, beyond the possible economic value of the contacts you can make are the simple pleasures of merely enjoying the company of others over a simple meal, a glass of beer, or a nice long walk. As the saying goes, the best things in life are free; these are the simple pleasures that so quickly become lost in the shuffle when we are focusing most of our waking hours on earning money.

If you don't want to start up a new group right now, or if you currently lack the contacts to do so, you may be able to find existing support groups of unemployed people in your local area. This is a great way to meet people, especially if you have recently relocated. You can find groups with similar interests or shared concerns on *www.meetup.com*. Their motto of "Do Something, Learn Something, Share Something, Change Something" is a perfect explanation for the purpose of an unemployed support group. Meetup.com already offers some existing groups for unemployed people that you can review at *www.unemployed.meetup.com*, but if there isn't a Meetup group that meets your needs or is located near you, you should consider starting one of your own. What a great way to build leadership skills while networking and performing a valuable service for other people going through a tough, often lonely, time!

POOLING RESOURCES WITH FRIENDS

One of the best forms of support you may receive from your friends is practical. You can save a lot of cold hard cash when you share living accommodations with a group of roommates—the more the better. Having been through college, you're probably already accustomed to sharing tight quarters, so this shouldn't be hard for you. In fact, it may even be enjoyable.

You've probably heard the saying that "two can live as cheaply as one." The same general principle is magnified with groups of three or more. You can cut your rent in half or less simply by inviting a friend or two to move in with you, and you gain companionship, to boot!

To really maximize the potential savings, you should also pool other expenses, such as food and staples, and buy them in bulk. It's expensive to buy tiny packages of food for one person, but when you have a larger group, you can save money by purchasing items in larger quantities. You will find that the economies of scale begin to kick in and you can really save some money. You can carpool together, cook together, rent movies together, share laundry, and even exchange clothes, if you're close in size. You can cook in larger quantities and invite your unemployment support group over to share in a free dinner, which will surely be appreciated by others pinching pennies. If you put your heads together, you will be able to come up with other ways to share costs and reduce your expenses.

EXPANDING YOUR EXISTING NETWORK

You probably already have a "passive" network of contacts. These are the people you know from high school and college, from your neighborhood, and because they are related to you. This is the core of your personal network, but you will want to be more active about expanding and growing your network, deliberately and systematically, in order to maximize your potential reach and increase the value of your contacts. First, you may want to make a formal list of everyone in your network, so that you are sure you aren't leaving anyone out. Include friends from K–12, community groups and religious organizations, past coworkers, and of course college friends and relatives.

What about including the parents of all your school friends and the friends of all your relatives? These are also potential allies, who could connect you to completely different demographic groups and who may be better positioned to hire, so be sure to reach out to them as you implement your networking plan, as well.

Consider shifting some of your friends from Facebook onto a LinkedIn account and establishing a more professional, career-focused presence there. Facebook is more for friendship, fun, and sharing, whereas LinkedIn has emerged as a better career-networking tool. One recent survey from Jobvite found that 93 percent of job recruiters check LinkedIn to find qualified candidates. This is far higher than the percentages of recruiters checking Facebook or Twitter, so take note and open an account immediately, if you haven't already done so. If you already have a LinkedIn account, devote some time to sprucing up your profile and building your network. You can even post recommendations and endorsements on LinkedIn. You could write some for your friends and acquaintances, and vice versa. Of course, this is more effective when you have done business together. Be sure to ask current or former bosses to post recommendations, too. This can be a very convincing part of your online presence.

Why not start a recommendation-writing campaign? The fact of the matter is that people are unlikely to give you an online recommendation unless you ask for one. So, pluck up your nerve and ask! One easy way to get the ball rolling would be to offer to write a recommendation for someone else, and then see if he offers to reciprocate, which most people will. Writing a recommendation doesn't cost you anything, other than a small amount of time, but it is sure to be appreciated and remembered forever by the recipient. Think of it as building social capital. Be generous with the number of recommendations you write, and be lavish in your praise, and you will find that others will respond the same way to your requests for recommendations.

Another way to build more connections is by joining community organizations such as Kiwanis, Moose, the Masons, Odd Fellows, Elks, Rotary, Sertoma, Optimists,

Knights of Columbus, or Shriners. In decades past, these fraternal organizations with the funny names (and sometimes silly hats) have served as vital networking avenues for generations of men and, more recently, women. Their populations have dwindled over the years and they are faced with aging leadership and declining membership. Suddenly, they recognize the need to welcome "young blood." This can be a great opportunity for you to jump into action and possibly assume leadership in an established organization with strong roots in your community. Many of these organizations do not actively recruit. To join, you have to reach out, express an interest, and speak to an existing member. Membership in these groups may be down, but they are still quite active and well connected in most communities. Most would welcome an enthusiastic new recruit and may be more than happy to turn over some leadership responsibilities. This is a great way to build positive visibility within your community.

The Kindness of Strangers

What about meeting complete strangers and adding them to your network? You can even accomplish this feat! As I already mentioned, informational interviews are a great way to reach out to strangers and turn them into personal contacts. The key is to approach these individuals with no ulterior motive other than to learn from them. Be sure to thank profusely any people gracious enough to offer you an informational interview and ask them if they know anyone else you should contact. Then invite the individuals to join your growing social network.

You can also meet people through business organizations, such as your local Chamber of Commerce, coworking groups, or local Meetups. You should consider joining these organizations, as well. All of these suggestions can provide ways for you to get out of your house and stay involved, even when you're not working. For now, consider attending meetings your full-time job.

There are professional associations for members of certain occupational fields. These can be particularly fruitful organizations to join, when you know what line of occupation you wish to pursue. Once you have narrowed down your professional interest, you should locate the organization representing members of this occupational field and join it, even if you're not yet working in the field. After all, you have to start somewhere, and a great place to begin is by meeting people already working in the field. Affiliating with the professional organization shows that you are sufficiently informed and involved to know the proper organization to join. It demonstrates that you value staying on top of the latest information enough to make the investment to belong, and it also demonstrates your initiative. Many professional organizations hold annual, national conferences that often function as recruiting events for members seeking new employees. If you're not involved, and if they don't know who you are, how can you expect them to notice you or think of you when openings occur? This is why it is so important to attend these events.

In between national events, many groups will hold local regional meetings, which can be great networking opportunities. Most professional organizations levy membership dues. I believe these are a worthwhile investment in your career and that it would be penny-wise, but pound foolish, to fail to join simply to save money. Sometimes, these organizations will even offer special introductory rates for new graduates or entry-level workers, so you may be able to receive discounted pricing. In most cases, the costs of joining will be tax deductible, so save your receipt.

Once you start doing your research, you may be astonished to discover the number of professional associations out there. The hardest part may be figuring out the best one to join! Let's see: there is the International Federation of Accountants, the Independent Insurance Agents of America, the Association of Information Technology Professionals, the National Society of Professional Engineers, the National Association of Environmental Professionals, the Society for Human Resource Management, the International Association of Business Communicators, and the United Professional Sales Association. The list goes on and on. I'm not recommending the particular associations; I'm simply pointing out that whatever your area of interest, there is probably an organization devoted to it that you should find out about. Some are devoted to serving certain segments of the population, such as the Society of Women Engineers and the National Organization of Minority Architects.

Most of these organizations function to educate members of the profession and also to uphold standards of ethics and performance within the profession for the good of all. You have to become familiar with an occupational field to learn the best organizations to join, which is why networking and informational interviewing can be so valuable. Even if an informational interviewing contact can't refer you to any job openings or contacts, she should at least be able to provide you with the names of organizations you could join to learn more. You could also ask professors in your academic department in college for their recommendations on the best professional organizations to join.

You can find a fairly comprehensive list of professional organizations on Yahoo! Directory at *www.dir.yahoo .com/business_and_economy/organizations/professional*. When you locate the right organization in your field and become actively involved, information will begin to spill and doors will begin to open for you. And why not? You will be informed and know what is going on!

Once you have located a promising organization, start volunteering to help with planning events and other administrative needs. Just as with alumni associations, those who raise their hand get recognized. Sign up to become involved on committees as you increase your involvement with the organization, and take those responsibilities seriously. The better job you do, the more you will attract positive notice. This can lead to letters of recommendation or valuable personal introductions. When you're unemployed, there are obviously places where you're going to have to economize, but don't be cheap about investing in professional memberships. Once you've located the right organization and determined that it is worthwhile, make the financial investment to join, even if it means cutting back elsewhere. Then, make the time commitment to attend regularly!

COWORKING TO BUILD CONNECTIONS . . . OR A BUSINESS

I discussed coworking earlier when I was talking about economic survival, but the social aspects of this working arrangement deserve more attention. Not only is coworking much more affordable than setting up a separate shop, but it also provides the camaraderie and sense of community that can be lacking for an independent entrepreneur. It can be a great way to expand your business connections.

A coworking arrangement can easily become the basis for a new business formation, as members recognize the mutual benefits they can gain from working together in a new enterprise, not to mention a steady source of motivation and social support for members. A typical coworking arrangement will develop a family atmosphere with shared events, business lunches, and after-hours social engagements.

If you can't find an existing coworking site in your local area, why not consider starting one? This could be a viable business idea for a motivated and visionary entrepreneur! The key to succeeding as a businessperson is to recognize an existing or growing need and then seek to fill it better than anyone else. Do you know any unemployed college

graduates who need affordable working accommodations, with networking capabilities and access to a printer
and photocopier? Space is often the biggest expense for a
struggling new entrepreneur. Many cash-strapped entrepreneurs would prefer to work out of an office, with a formal business address, than out of their homes. It presents
a more professional image, especially when meeting with
clients. Can you figure out a way to provide it at a low cost,
while retaining a profit for yourself?

You wouldn't have to start large; you could begin with
just one other entrepreneur in a home office or even a converted basement or garage (think Steve Jobs and Woz),
and eventually move into a rented space. As you find more
interested coworkers, you could rent a larger office space
and then advertise for others to join your growing group.
You would, of course, collect a fee for your managerial and
marketing duties. While you may start out as a freelancer
who needed a worksite, your focus could eventually shift
into becoming a business owner who provides office solutions for others needing low-cost office space.

The coworking model can fit nicely with revitalization
plans in many deteriorated downtown areas and become
a real asset to a community. By reclaiming an abandoned
or poorly maintained property and investing elbow grease
and ingenuity, coworking sites can provide an extremely
affordable working alternative for a large number of people
while bringing business back to a stagnating neighborhood. By organizing educational workshops for the members of the coworking group, you could also perform a
valuable public service.

Often, the best way to help yourself is to start by helping others. Think first of what others need and how you could provide useful services to help other people meet those needs. There is probably nothing more satisfying than doing well while also doing good.

CHAPTER SEVEN

THE LIGHT AT THE END OF THE TUNNEL

"Demography is destiny."
—Auguste Comte

You may not have graduated at the best moment in history, but maybe your timing wasn't so bad, after all. In fact, the long-term employment picture for young people is actually shaping up to be very bright, indeed. Believe it or not, demographic forces are aligning to create what looks to be a phenomenal seller's job market in the not-so-distant future.

The American workforce is aging, and the oldest members of the numerous Baby Boomer generation have already begun to retire. Because the Baby Boom was so large, this means that there are more soon-to-be-retiring Boomers than younger workers to replace them, which should lead to future labor shortages. And that means jobs.

Year to year, the economy may be good or bad, but as the father of sociology Auguste Comte famously pointed out: "Demography is destiny." This means that huge, statistical forces such as birth rates and death rates shape the future far more powerfully and predictably than mere economic ones.

The coming workforce changes are an inevitable part of the greatest demographic change in human history. It is difficult to overstate the magnitude of what is coming, since we've never experienced anything quite like this before. The oldest of the 76+ million Baby Boomers began reaching the traditional retirement age of sixty-five in 2011. As these Boomers cycle out of the workforce, the younger cohorts behind them are significantly smaller. Most commentators point out what these changes will mean for Social Security, but few mention what hopeful news this is for younger people waiting to find good jobs. Every older person who retires leaves an opening and a need for a younger person to assume his or her vacated position. This is great news!

For the past several decades Americans have been having fewer children and living longer. The result is that what used to be a demographic pyramid with a small number of elderly at the top and a wide base of many children at the bottom has been altered.

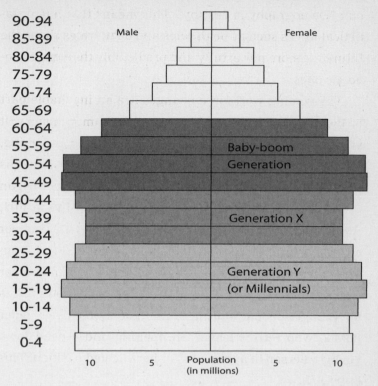

Current United States Population

	Male	Female	
90-94			
85-89			
80-84			
75-79			
70-74			
65-69			
60-64			
55-59		Baby-boom	
50-54		Generation	
45-49			
40-44			
35-39		Generation X	
30-34			
25-29			
20-24		Generation Y	
15-19		(or Millennials)	
10-14			
5-9			
0-4			

10   5   Population   5   10
                    (in millions)

As you can see, we actually have a contraction in the middle of our current demographic chart, with more older than younger people in certain age categories—a startling and unprecedented development. Because of the "baby bust" and the "birth dearth" of the 1970s and early 1980s, we will soon be moving into a period of a declining number of working-age citizens. Generation X, which follows the Boomers, is only half the previous generation's size, at about 46 million.

This represents a huge opportunity for those younger people following the long-suffering, long-overshadowed Generation Xers. When Boomers finally retire, we can expect to see plentiful job opportunities for those prepared to take them. You've probably heard the proverb, "It's always darkest before the dawn." Well, right now the economy and your individual job prospects may look fairly gray, with the older generations overshadowing the younger ones, but things are about to get a whole lot brighter.

BY THE NUMBERS

Baby Boomers currently represent about half of the entire U.S. workforce. This is slightly more than the number of workers from the succeeding two generations combined. As 76 million Baby Boomers leave the workforce, there will be twice as many retirees as there are today, but only 18 percent more workers. Meanwhile, the number of workers between the ages of thirty-five and forty-four is projected to decrease by 10 percent. So there is a lot for you to be optimistic about in terms of coming supply and demand in the labor market.

$

The facts are irrefutable: 10,000 Baby Boomers turn sixty-five every day—a pattern that will continue for the next eighteen *years*. It is true that some of them are trying to delay their retirements, but the overall trend is unstoppable and inevitable. Someone is eventually going to have to fill those emptying positions. Likewise, these retiring Boomers will in turn create a huge, growing demand for the predictable services that retirees consume, including health care, recreation, financial management, and so on.

There is an old saying that goes, "If you don't like the weather, just wait." The same principle applies to the economy because it is always changing. The long-term demographic odds are heavily stacked in your favor, if you can just hunker down and wait for the current employment dry spell to pass, while preparing yourself for coming opportunities. Soon, it could be raining jobs. It would be very premature for you to give up on your employment prospects just yet, with such optimistic trends beginning to emerge.

THE UNEMPLOYMENT RACE

You may not have the fastest time out of the starting block of life, but you may be hitting your career stride when opportunities are excellent! In many ways, your timing may be ideal. It is far easier to weather a period of temporary unemployment when you are young and can keep your expenses lower. Think how difficult it is to endure unemployment as a middle-aged adult, with a family to support and a mortgage to pay, during what are supposed to be your peak earning years before retirement.

It is far too early to count your generation out of the employment race. In fact, the race is just getting started for your age group. It is going to be a marathon rather than a sprint, so it won't hurt you to pace yourself in the beginning. Furthermore, if your generation is really going to have a longer lifespan than previous generations—some say with a life expectancy of ninety—then a few years of early underemployment are a matter of little consequence in the overall scheme of things.

WHERE ARE THE JOBS GOING?

The advice that "demography is destiny" should give you some very good clues as to where demand is going to be highest in the coming decades. In any economy, there is always work that has to be done; the trick is figuring out where the greatest needs are and anticipating where future needs will emerge. If you review the demographic chart above, you can make many fairly reliable predictions about the future. For instance, the Baby Boom cohort will soon retire and then they will become elderly. They will begin spending their accumulated retirement assets on the typical purchases made by older consumers, such as recreational travel, restaurant meals, entertainment, retirement community housing and services, financial advice, and, of course, health care. Beyond the traditional medical services, you can anticipate a growing demand for assistive products such as better glasses, hearing aids, and mobility devices. It is likely that they will seek out alternative health therapies as well, so those could be promising fields to investigate. Many older people will eventually need assisted-living services, so there should be a huge, growing need for home health-care services. Seek ways to predict and meet this coming consumer demand and you may be able to find great economic success!

Furthermore, after you move past the contraction in the middle of the demographic chart, you notice another bulge in the population, which represents the "Baby Boomlet" (children of the Baby Boomers), plus additional immigrants. As this cohort ages, you can expect to see a rise in all the sorts of typical consumer spending associated with a large middle-aged population in their peak spending years, including housing, furnishings, and purchases for their own children. This should be good news for the overall economy and drive economic growth in the future.

To make even more reliable predictions about where the opportunities are likely to be brightest in coming years, you will want to access the government's own statistics and compiled data. Visit *www.careerinfonet.org*, which uses information from the U.S. Department of Labor, to find the projected numbers of openings for various positions through 2018. I've already shown you the top jobs at any level of education, and the list of top jobs requiring some postsecondary training. Now, here's the list of jobs predicted to have the most openings at the bachelor's degree (or higher) level.

Table 7.1

Occupation	Number of openings, nationally
1. Elementary school teacher	59,650
2. Postsecondary (college) teacher	55,290
3. General and operations managers	50,220
4. Accountants and auditors	49,750
5. Secondary school teacher	41,240
6. Management analyst	30,650
7. Physicians and surgeons	26,050
8. Middle school teacher	25,110
9. Lawyers	24,040
10. Computer systems analysts	22,280
11. Computer application engineers	21,840
12. Clergy	21,770
13. Computer software engineers, systems	15,340
14. Financial managers	13,820

Table 7.1	
Occupation	Number of openings, nationally
15. Construction managers	13,770
16. Market research analysts	13,730
17. Computer systems administrators	13,550
18. Public relations specialists	13,130
19. Securities, financial services sales agents	12,680
20. Sales managers	12,660

I've cited a lot of facts and figures in this book, including the table above. However, don't just accept information or predictions on faith and then make major life decisions based on a single article or statistic. Each piece of information will contribute to your growing understanding of job prospects in different fields. You should then continue to conduct research until you begin to form your own firm convictions about the smartest career moves for you to make, based on the best available data. That's the best anyone can do.

Become a trendspotter. I believe this has never been more important, since the entire global economy is in such a state of major transition right now. You have already picked up this book, which shows that you are actively looking for answers. This shows a lot of initiative. I hope you will keep looking for additional advice and continue reading economic trend research throughout your career. This is the safest route to ensure that you will never be completely blindsided by major shifts and will be able to spot new, emerging trends in time to profit from them.

For instance, in the book *The Lights in the Tunnel,* Martin Ford, the founder of a Silicon Valley software firm, offers some informed guesses about where the overall economy is heading. He comments on the growing problem of outsourced knowledge worker jobs, which can often be digitally sent overseas, and the increasing appeal of jobs that can't be sent offshore, wirelessly. As we've already discussed, this includes many kinds of hands-on work. Ford expects that there is "likely to be a migration toward relatively skilled blue collar jobs if there is a perception that these occupations offer more security." He argues that workers will "increasingly turn to the trades. As we have seen, jobs for people like auto mechanics, truck drivers, plumbers and so forth are among the most difficult to automate."

This is the sort of insight that can help you plan for your future amidst considerable uncertainty. Even if you don't plan on becoming an auto mechanic yourself, perhaps you could still find ways to profit from this trend, perhaps by providing services to workers in these industries. Don't just read, however. Put on your thinking cap and ask yourself what the information you are learning means for you and how you may want to adapt your behavior to adjust to changing economic circumstances.

A few other suggestions, to get a sense of where the jobs and overall economy are heading, are *Aftershock* by Robert B. Reich, *Aftershock* (yes, that's the same title!) by

David Wiedemer, and *The Third Industrial Revolution* by Jeremy Rifkin. These books can help you understand the seismic transformation that is currently taking place and prepare you to find your place in a radically altered economy. You will need to pay ongoing attention to developing trends and continue to be on the lookout for new sources of information as the economy continues to shift and as some once-secure jobs become more precarious. As Reid Hoffman and Ben Casnocha argue in *The Start-Up of You*, you need to remain in a state of "Permanent Beta," in which your career planning is never finished, and you remain alert for the next round of improvements and adjustments to make. This is the best way to ensure that you remain relevant, adaptable, and employable throughout your entire career.

So, it's not all bad news out there. There are still opportunities to find jobs, sometimes in unexpected places, even during the worst economy since the Great Depression. By being alert and informed, you will be able to uncover possibilities that may elude other members of your generation. Furthermore, the demographic forces that are currently restricting your economic opportunities will soon be shifting to make future job opportunities much more plentiful. There is every reason to remain optimistic and to continue to make plans to prepare for a bright career with an employer or to become your own employer by starting a new business or growing an existing one.

CONCLUSION

It's time to take action. Let's review your survival plan, so that you have a clear roadmap to escape the unemployment dead end and get back on the path to a good job.

First, check your mindset. To survive emotionally as an unemployed college graduate, you're going to have to discard any bitterness and leave it behind. Accept that this is how things are right now, rather than wishing they were different. Resolve to make the most of your existing opportunities, no matter how humble.

This means you're going to have to overcome the unhelpful attitude that some types of work are "beneath" a college graduate or that you "deserve" something. An attitude like that can only hold you back. Remember: no one owes you anything. You simply can't expect to rest on your laurels in a tough economy. Broaden your definition of a good job and where you will live for the time being. Being flexible will reveal hidden possibilities.

Your short-term plan is to do whatever you need to do to pay your bills, while your long-term plan is to seek opportunities to turn your survival gig into a full-time career with advancement potential, find ways to get noticed by a desirable employer, or start your own business enterprise. Along the way, pay attention to what is going on in the wider economy, so that you will be able to spot emerging trends and act on them.

Perhaps one of the wisest sayings to keep in mind along the way is, *This, too, shall pass.* Your current circumstances, for better or for worse, are transitory. Don't get too sad when life throws you a curveball like unemployment, because good fortune probably lies beyond the next corner. Likewise, don't get too cocky when you are on top, because life has a way of humbling the mighty. Those who shoulder unemployment with equanimity and good humor, while growing their skill set, will emerge best positioned to profit greatly when the economy rebounds, as it inevitably will.

The famous chemist Louis Pasteur proclaimed, "Fortune favors the prepared." By this, he meant that when you are ready for something good to happen, suddenly you see all sorts of opportunities and new ideas. Your luck changes! Ongoing preparation is going to be critical to your success once the economy rebounds.

You must stay engaged. If one employment door will not open for you, look for another door or for a side entrance. Still no luck? Then keep knocking and see if anyone left a window unlatched! Persistence and thoroughness can work wonders in most endeavors in life, the same way that water can wear down stone.

Your future is still bright. Optimism, persistence, and steady action will see you successfully through this low point in your earning career and will continue to serve you well once you gain career momentum. Don't let anyone— like a hiring manager—or anything—like an economic recession—stop you from moving forward toward your ultimate career goal. With a good plan, a refreshingly positive attitude, and determination, you will find ways to excel and achieve success even in a downturn. Hard work counts for a lot, too; it can overcome almost any obstacle and open almost any door. A little good luck never hurt anyone, either, so allow me to wish you the very best of luck in your job hunt. Now, get out there and make things happen!

RECOMMENDED RESOURCES

ONLINE SOURCES

State Job Centers

www.statelocalgov.net/50states-jobs.cfm
www.careeronestop.org
www.careerinfonet.org

Career Testing

Myers Briggs Career Test:
   www.humanmetrics.com/cgi-win/jtypes2.asp
Credentials Center:
   www.careeronestop.org/credentialing/
   credentialinghome.asp

List of Business and Professional Organizations

www.dir.yahoo.com/business_and_economy/organizations/professional

Coworking

www.wiki.coworking.info/w/page/16583831/frontpage
www.loosecubes.com
www.nextspace.us
www.opendesks.com
www.the-hub.net

Starting a Business

www.score.org
www.sba.gov

Health Insurance

www.healthcare.gov
www.pennyhealthinsurance.com
www.vimo.com
www.ehealthinsurance.com
www.younginvincibles.org

Student Loan Repayment

www.nslds.ed.gov/nslds_SA
www.studentaid.ed.gov
www.finaid.org
http://studentloanjustice.org

Saving Money

www.101waystosavemoney.com
www.beingfrugal.net
www.freecycle.org

Comparing Places to Live

www.bestplaces.net

Foodstamp Prescreening Eligibility Tool

www.snap-step1.usda.gov/fns

Foodstamp Information

www.ssa.gov/pubs/10101.html or 1-800-772-1213

Therapists

www.therapists.psychologytoday.com

National Suicide Prevention Hotline

1-800-273-TALK (8255)

PRINT REFERENCES

Allen, Charlotte. "A Terrible Time for New Ph.D.s." *Minding the Campus.com*, February 3, 2011.

Alonso-Zaldivar, Ricardo. "Obama admin: 2.5M young adults gain coverage." *Excite News*, December 14, 2011.

Cass, Connie. "Health care options for young, healthy and broke." *Yahoo! Finance*, July, 10, 2012.

Cohen, Patricia. "Doctoral Candidates Anticipate Hard Times." *The New York Times*, March 6, 2009.

Couch, Christina. "10 Top Telecommuting Jobs to Live Abroad." *Yahoo! Finance*, August 23, 2012.

Cowan, Claudia. "On the job hunt: machinists in high demand." *FoxNews.com*, December 15, 2011.

Crawford, Matthew B. *Shop Class as Soulcraft: An Inquiry into the Value of Work.* New York: The Penguin Press, 2009.

Davidson, Paul. "Temp workers' numbers climbing in rocky economy." *USA Today*, July 7, 2012.

Education News. *The Higher Education Bubble.* Available at: *www.educationnews.org/ higher-education-bubble.*

Egan, Dermot. "Co-working puts the spark back into office life." *The Guardian*, December 22, 2011.

Ellis, Blake. "Double your salary in the middle of Nowhere, North Dakota." CNNMoney, December 20, 2011.

Ford, Martin. *The Lights in the Tunnel: Automation, Accelerating Technology and the Economy of the Future.* USA: CreateSpace, 2009.

Godofsky, M. P. P., C. Zukin, and C. Van Horn. *Unfulfilled Expectations: Recent College Graduates Struggle in a Troubled Economy.* New Jersey: John J. Heldrich Center for Workforce Development, 2011.

Goozner, Merrill. "The Ten Best Cities to Find a Job." *The Fiscal Times*, December 7, 2011.

Hoffman, Reid, and Ben Casnocha. *The Start-Up of You: Adapt to the Future, Invest in Yourself, and Transform Your Career.* New York: Crown Business, 2012.

Leslie, Jerold. "Best Places for Starting Over in 2012." *Yahoo! Finance*, December 19, 2011.

Michalowicz, Mike. *The Toilet Paper Entrepreneur: The Tell-It-Like-It-Is Guide to Cleaning Up in Business, Even If You Are at the End of Your Roll.* USA: Obsidian Launch, LLC, 2008.

Morello, Carol. "More college-educated jump tracks to become skilled manual laborers." *The Washington Post*, June 15, 2010.

Palazzolo, Joe. "Law grads face brutal job market." *The Wall Street Journal*, June 25, 2012.

Palazzolo, Joe, and Jennifer Smith. "Law school wins in graduate suit." *The Wall Street Journal*, March 22, 2012.

Pew Social and Demographic Trends. "The Return of the Multi-Generational Family Household." Washington, DC: Pew Research Center, March 18, 2010.

Staley, Willy. "Two maps that show why grads are screwed." *My Band Tracker*, May 31, 2012.

U.S. Congress Joint Economic Committee. *Understanding the Economy: Unemployment Among Young Workers*, May 2010.

Weitzman, Hal, and Robin Harding. "Skills gap hobbles U.S. employers." *Financial Times*, December 13, 2011.

Whitney, Lance. "Heads up, LinkedIn users: 93% of recruiters are looking at you." *CNet News*, July 10, 2012.